THE "UNHOLY" APOSTLES

Shipwreck Tales
of the
Apostle Islands

by
James M. Keller

Printed by
Sheridan Books
Chelsea, MI 48118

First Printing 1984
Second Printing 1985
Third Printing 1989
Fourth Printing 1993
Fifth Printing 2000

Cover art by Edward Pusick

PRINTED IN THE UNITED STATES OF AMERICA

ISBN 0-933577-001

DEDICATION

This book is lovingly dedicated to two of the finest people I have ever known. Like the infinite power of the sea and the gentle wind that lifts the sagging sail, they have been a constant source of strength and hope to me through the years. This work is dedicated to Dr. Paul and Marguerite Keller. . . my parents.

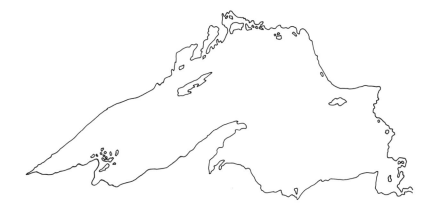

These grand fresh-water seas of ours...possess an ocean-like expansiveness. They are swept by Borean and dismasting waves as direful as any that lash the salted wave. They know what shipwrecks are; for, out of sight of land, however inland, they have drowned many a midnight ship with all its shrieking crew.

"Ishmael" in Herman Melville's **Moby Dick**

TABLE OF CONTENTS

ACKNOWLEDGEMENTS

It is with a sincere note of appreciation that I acknowledge the following people and institutions. Their kind offers of assistance were truly invaluable to me while compiling this book. I wish to extend my deepest thanks to each and every one of them.

Don Albrecht of the Bayfield Heritage Association

John Chapple of the Ashland Daily Press

Phil Green

James Hansen of the Wisconsin State Historical Society

Thom Holden of the Canal Park Marine Museum

Larry W. Hoopman

Richard Keller

C. Patrick Labadie of the Canal Park Marine Museum

Ernie LaPointe

Norma Lien of the Bayfield Heritage Association

Edward Pusick

Ralph K. Roberts

Ken E. Thro

Jane Tolliver of the Ashland Historical Society

Dr. Julius F. Wolff Jr.

Richard J. Wright

Vaughn Public Library

Delta County Historical Society

Marine Historical Society of Detroit

Marquette County Historical Society

Milwaukee Public Library

University of Detroit

A special note of appreciation is due Ms. Teresa Keller. Without her help this book may never have been completed.

FOREWARD

"The 'Unholy' Apostles" deals with a decidedly grim subject in Lake Superior lore — the shipwreck. The setting is the beautiful Chequamegon Bay area on the south shore. The time frame runs roughly from 1870 to 1930. Within this sixty year period Apostle Island waters witnessed many a troubled vessel, and produced a plethora of interesting tales.

Shipwrecks have long fascinated mankind. After all, what's more dramatic than a vessel being lost at sea? Shipwreck tales seem to spark the imagination, or perhaps they massage the morbid side of human curiosity. Man's seemingly timeless struggle with the sea has long been considered high adventure. Battling the elements — whether it be storm-swelled seas, raging fire, or thick fog — is often brought to its most basic form aboard a ship: sink or swim, survive or die. Sometimes man is victorious: he conquers his unexpected adversary or is at least granted reprieve. The following tales concern those times when he wasn't.

The stories contained in this book are basically historical accounts. Dates, names, locations and sizes have been presented as accurately as possible. As with any dramatic subject however, the "adventure" enters in. Along with the factual history comes ample amounts of heroics, sacrifice, cowardice and courage.

The book is broken up into three sections. Chapters dealing with pre-1900 shipwrecks comprise Section I, while Section II includes wrecks occurring after the turn of the century. A third section deals with maritime accidents, abandonments, and "visiting the vessels" today. Footnotes follow each story and a bibliography and index conclude the book.

INTRODUCTION

The Chequamegon Bay Region today is widely recognized for its excellent recreational opportunities. In years past though, this vicinity was actually considered an important shipping area. At one time Ashland was one of the busiest freshwater ports in the nation and the Apostle Islands were literally brimming with activity.

From the 1870's up to the Great Depression era Chequamegon Bay was a major center for commerce. For decades ships plied these waters: the long forgotten sidewheelers, the graceful schooners, the powerful little tugs, the wooden bulk freighters, and eventually the bigger steel steamers. The volume of vessel traffic operating in the area during its heyday was immense. And, like other major maritime regions, these waters witnessed their fair share of accidents.

The "dead" ships that sit scattered about the Apostle Island area are part of the legacy of that great shipping period. Victims of fog, fire and fate they lay as mute testimony to the power and potential danger of Lake Superior. Tugs, towbarges, schooners and steamers have all unfortunately foundered and found bottom in these waters.

The possible hazards facing the Superior sailor in the region were many. Unwary ships slicing through fog sometimes stranded on an Apostle shoal. A November northeaster often sent ships scurrying for shelter, and the islands could either prove to be haven or hell for storm-driven skippers. Devastating blazes which devoured vessels sometimes took their toll before the crew could react.

The great shipping days for this area are all but gone now. The big boats rarely venture into the bay anymore. Some still deliver coal to the Ashland dock and some may venture into the lee of an island waiting out a storm. Others might moor at the defunct oredock while the Duluth harbor traffic lightens up. But these occasions are uncommon. The last vestiges of that bygone era can still be seen however. Glimpses of it are offered in the bones of the vessels lying near shore, in Ashland's shallow water pilings protruding above the water's surface, and sometimes in the tone of the old local mariner's voice when he begins his story "I remember when..."

SECTION I

Pre 1900 Shipwrecks

D.R. OWEN
The First...
MANISTEE
A Ship of Many Mysteries
OZAUKEE
A Bad River Battering
PRUSSIA
A Lightkeeper's Heroism
LUCERNE
Frozen Death
CITY OF ASHLAND
The Namesake Ship
MARY CARGAN
Victim of Impatience?!
M.R. WARNER
Slowly...But Surely
ANTELOPE
A Name With A Curse
R.G. STEWART
A Packet Steamer Peril

Pre 1900 Era

The Chequamegon region of the late 1800's was, in a sense, a microcosm of Lake Superior in general. Activity in the area grudgingly but gradually began. Once it reached a certain point however, it literally erupted. Growth was the catchword and commerce was the key.

Originally Madeline Island was the focal point of all local activities. As more people moved into the area however, expansion to the mainland became inevitable. Fishing, trapping and trading gradually gave way to other forms of economic endeavor. The early 1870's witnessed the railroad's arrival to this region, and with it a rapid increase of business and population. Ashland — for many years kept alive by a single family — suddenly started growing. Sawmills began popping up along the waterfront, followed by coal docks and an oredock in 1884. Bayfield expanded: R.D. Pike built a sawmill south of town and the fishing industry grew. Washburn was born in 1883. By the end of the century Chequamegon Bay was

A "bird's eye view" of Bayfield in 1886.   Bayfield Heritage Association

thriving, and Ashland had established itself as a major freshwater port.

The region's exports included lumber, iron ore, fish and brownstone. Coal was constantly shipped in to fire the mines and the factories. Small packet steamers continually brought general merchandise and more people to the area.

The vessels operating in the region were a diverse mixture of sailboats and steamers. Early on the great sailing ships ruled the waters. Tugs became increasingly prevalent to raft the fallen timber and move schooners in and out of docks. Wooden bulk steamers began appearing with greater frequency, and by century's end the big steel freighter definitively foretold the future shipping era. Packet steamers moved passengers and diverse cargos along regularly-run routes. Excursion boats and ferries moved around the islands daily and fishing vessels and private yachts were in abundance.

The period from 1870 to 1899 was truly remarkable in terms of growth. Originally little more than a handful of villagers, by century's end the Chequamegon Bay was a bustling, busy harbor.

A "bird's eye view" of Ashland in 1890. Ashland Historical Society

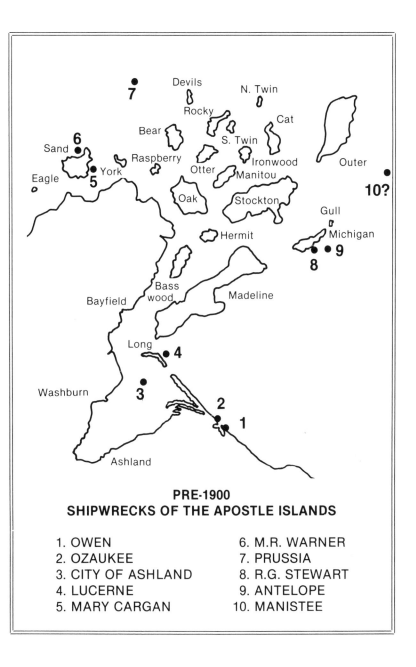

PRE-1900
SHIPWRECKS OF THE APOSTLE ISLANDS

1. OWEN
2. OZAUKEE
3. CITY OF ASHLAND
4. LUCERNE
5. MARY CARGAN

6. M.R. WARNER
7. PRUSSIA
8. R.G. STEWART
9. ANTELOPE
10. MANISTEE

D.R. OWEN
The First...

In the early 1870's the Chequamegon Bay area was, for the most part, heavily wooded wilderness. Bayfield and LaPointe were small villages consisting of traders, trappers and fishermen. Washburn did not yet exist, and Ashland was a tiny town with no real premonition of its upcoming economic boom. There were a handful of budding entrepreneurs around however, who saw the logging activity moving westward and realized the moneymaking possibilities in the region. One of these was a man named W.R. Sutherland, who built the first sawmill in Ashland. With the "Ashland Lumber Company" underway, Sutherland was in need of some form of transport for his product.[1] For this purpose he leased the 100 foot schooner D.R. OWEN and began operating one of the first cargo-carrying vessels based in Ashland. The D.R. OWEN also claims another "first": it holds the dubious distinction of being the first documented shipwreck in the Chequamegon area.

A good share of Sutherland's early business consisted of transporting lumber to Isle Royale. A sawmill was not an economically feasible operation at Isle Royale at that time, so Sutherland provided the cut lumber to the mining camps and fishing interests that were springing up there. It was on a stormy voyage from Isle Royale to Ashland that the OWEN unfortunately took her place in Chequamegon shipping history.

On the morning of Thursday, September 6th, 1874 the OWEN departed the island after delivering a load of lumber. At 4:00 p.m. the wind that had been filling the schooner's sails completely died. A dead calm set in and the vessel drifted on the open lake for several hours. Sometime after nightfall a northeast breeze picked up and continued to grow stronger with each passing hour. Eventually the wind was blowing with tremendous force and a terrible storm ensued. The waves grew in size and a gale-driven downpour reduced visibility to zero. The schooner was taking a beating in the unsheltered seas, but seemed to be holding its own. Unfortunately for Sutherland and his crew, fate would soon turn against them.

Checking below deck one crewmember discovered a leak in

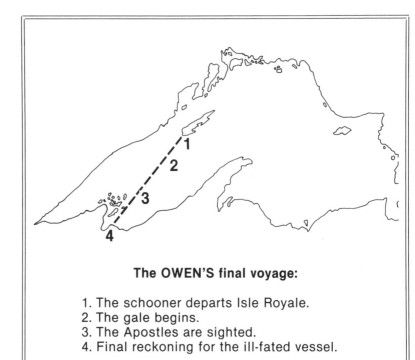

The OWEN'S final voyage:

1. The schooner departs Isle Royale.
2. The gale begins.
3. The Apostles are sighted.
4. Final reckoning for the ill-fated vessel.

the hull. Shortly after that the howling gale completely wrecked the OWEN'S partially reefed sails. Waves began crashing over the deck without respite. The crew now found themselves in the middle of a Lake Superior tempest with virtually no defenses. Realizing that the schooner was completely at the mercy of the storm gods, the men performed the only task they could: they lashed themselves to their posts.

Tied to the wheel, the masts and the rigging the men at least knew that they would not be blown off the ship or washed overboard. The furious storm raged on for what must have seemed an eternity. Friday came and went with little or no change in the weather. Saturday dawned and still the cursed gale would not blow itself out. The long hours passed until — miraculously — the Apostles were sighted! The mighty northeaster had blown the waterlogged OWEN in the right direction at least. The boat was still afloat and now, out of the darkness, a faint ray of hope had appeared!

Michigan Island loomed larger as the minutes marched on. The waves however, were still far too high for any real possibility of steering the schooner to safety. Finally at 4:00 p.m. on Saturday — a full forty eight hours after leaving land

— the OWEN reached terra firma once more. She was thrown onto the mainland very close to the mouth of the Bad River. The entire crew successfully managed to escape the broken vessel and crawl to safe ground. The terrifying ordeal — and the OWEN'S sailing days — had come to a close.

Sutherland and his exhausted crew walked to the Indian village of Odanah, and procured a canoe. With the storm subsiding they paddled on to Ashland via the Kakagon slough. The men could certainly consider themselves lucky having escaped the Superior storm with their lives. The unlucky OWEN was pounded to pieces, filled with sand, and written off as a total loss. And so ended the first chapter in the long history of Chequamegon shipwrecks...

Footnotes

1. The Ashland Lumber Company owned by Sutherland should not be confused with a later business of the same name. The second company (of which Sutherland had no part) began operating in the 1880's, and was quite successful for a good many years.

MANISTEE
A Ship of Many Mysteries

But hark! What shriek of death comes in the gale?
And in the distant ray what gleaming sail
Bends to the storm? Now sink the note of fear,
Ah, wretched mariners! no more shall day
Unclose his cheering eye to light ye on your way!

Bayfield County Press
(poem preceding article
concerning MANISTEE'S loss)

A good many mysteries surround the tragic loss of the steamer MANISTEE. She was one of those vessels that "went missing," a ship that Superior chose to claim and then give little clue as to how it happened. Questions concerning her "death" will undoubtedly remain forever unanswered. With no witnesses to the tragedy and all on board being killed, discussions concerning her loss can only end in speculation. Over a century later we know little more than what the Bayfield paper reported in 1883 — only "the sad certainty that the popular boat and her genial officers embarked for the sealess shores of eternity."[1]

The many riddles that surround the MANISTEE'S loss are intriguing. Perhaps the most pressing puzzle concerns the manner in which she went down — and there are many possibilities. Some seamen felt that the boat's boilers blew, thereby rendering her helpless in the high seas. Others felt that the heavy cargo load suddenly listed and she rolled to one side. Some thought the old vessel's hull was probably rotted and the pounding waves literally broke her to bits. Many people decided that the storm-enraged seas simply swallowed the steamer. The exact location of the sinking was never determined. It is not even known how many lives were lost in the accident — twenty three or twenty nine? Did the crew have time to abandon ship before she went down? Was there really a secret cargo on board worth a considerable amount of money, as was rumored? The unsolved riddles remain.[2]

The MANISTEE was a well-known vessel around the big

lake. She was a packet steamer which carried a variety of cargo and passengers along a regular south shore route. Under the guidance of the respected skipper John McKay the MANISTEE seemed to have that intangible "something" which made her a favorite around the region.

The MANISTEE had endured a long and interesting career before she went down. She was built in Cleveland by E.M. Peck in 1867. Originally owned by the Engelman Line of Milwaukee, the vessel ran between her home port and namesake city — Milwaukee to Manistee. In 1871 she was cut amidships and given an additional thirty feet, making her 184 feet long with a 677 gross tonnage.[3] That shipping season, having inherited the year round route between Milwaukee and Grand Haven, the MANISTEE found herself locked in an ice field for fifty eight days during one stretch. She came to Duluth in 1872 and eventually ended up running for the Leopold and Austrian Line, her final owners. During the last eleven years of her life her condition was alternately criticized and praised by steamboat inspectors and vesselmen alike.

The MANISTEE'S final voyage began at Duluth on Saturday, November 10th, 1883. She was bound for Ontonogan with a twenty three man crew and seven passengers. Her 400 ton cargo included large amounts of flour, mill goods, doors, sashes, furniture and general merchandise. Shortly after leaving port a nasty northwest gale descended upon the western lake. McKay and the MANISTEE fought their way to the Apostles and elected to seek shelter in Bayfield on Sunday the 11th.

The storm continued for days without letting up. An anxious McKay waited, watched the weather, and waited some more. On Thursday evening, the fifth day of his Bayfield stay, the captain decided there was sufficient sign of approaching good weather and ordered the MANISTEE'S departure at 8:40 p.m. It turned out to be a fatal decision. A local mariner, John A. Jacobs, later recounted this story:

> I was in Bayfield the night she left on that last fateful trip. I was aboard the MANISTEE for about an hour, visiting with the crew, as I was acquainted with nearly all of them. I was on the dock when McKay gave a blast of the whistle to let go the lines, and I can see her now backing out from the shelter of that dock and into that fearful storm. The MANISTEE was no fit boat to be out on Lake Superior in a storm like that, loaded to the guards as she was. The passenger's cabin was filled with furniture making her topheavy...I never saw Captain McKay again. The MANISTEE went to the bottom of Lake Superior with every soul aboard.[4]

A painting of the popular vessel MANISTEE. Bayfield Heritage Association

The "sufficiently good weather" that the MANISTEE steamed out in was later called "the worst storm ever seen on Lake Superior."[5] A possible vindication of McKay's "weather eye" though, is the fact that at approximately 10:00 p.m. two vessels which had also been holed up at Bayfield left port, bound for the Keweenaw Peninsula. The CITY OF DULUTH, which luckily had taken some of the MANISTEE'S passengers (although it is not certain how many), and the CHINA followed the same route as the ill-fated packet steamer. They survived the terrible blow, but never saw the MANISTEE on their way. Conjecture at the time had the MANISTEE clearing the islands, but turning around for Bayfield after finding the weather so bad. Of course, nobody will ever know exactly what happened. In any event, McKay, the MANISTEE and her men sailed into history that November day in 1883.

For months after the tragedy the MANISTEE'S wreckage appeared all over Lake Superior. On November 19th the first pieces from the lost ship were discovered. The tug MAYTHAM found part of the pilot house, some charcoal, and a bucket with the name "Manistee" on it. Less than a week later the V. SWAIN sailed through a field of wreckage by Copper Harbor which included furniture and foodstuffs. Near the Apostles the steamer OSCEOLA recovered barrels of flour and other bits of cargo the next day.

The entire Keweenaw Peninsula was literally littered with general merchandise from the MANISTEE for months. Everything from barrels of eggs, butter and flour to a passenger's trunk, a keg of whiskey and oars floated ashore. At Union Bay near the Porcupine Mountains the vessel's wheel and the unique gold eagle from the pilothouse were discovered. The MANISTEE'S mast was recovered at Sand Bay, and wreckage even started appearing at Isle Royale, Caribou Island and Point Mamainse. Bits and pieces of the boat were turning up everywhere, and yet strangely enough, no bodies were ever found.

Still later, two more interesting pieces of "wreckage" were discovered. The Ashland newspaper carried a story in November 1884 concerning a local fish dealer. Alphonse Lebel reported a lake trout being caught in the Apostles with a spoon in his stomach. Printed on the silver spoon was the word "Manistee."

An even more bizarre incident occurred the following summer. On May 24th, 1884 an Ashland local was strolling along the mouth of Fish Creek on Chequamegon Bay. Augustus Archambault happened to spot a bottle floating near the shore. A note inside the bottle read: "This is the MANISTEE, in a fearful storm. May not live to see morning. Ever yours to the world. John McKay, Capt." As with everything concerning the MANISTEE'S loss, the validity of the note remains a mystery.

The MANISTEE caught in an icefield, a situation which she endured for fifty eight days one winter. Ken Thro Collection

Two people who were very familiar with John McKay's signature felt the note was genuine. C.J. Higgins of the Wisconsin Central Railroad saw McKay sign for cargo many times, and decided that it was his handwriting. The harbor collector at Ashland, Mr. J. Bowen, also claimed the note was authentic!

Contrary opinion concerning the note's authenticity was offered by the ASHLAND NEWS. They decided that the entire affair was a hoax, and editorialized:

> There is work for the fool killer in the vicinity of Ashland. Some idiot prepared a bottle in which he placed a note purporting to have been written by Captain John McKay of the lost steamer MANISTEE. The bottle was picked up from the beach near Ashland this weekend and the details of the MANISTEE horror revived by sensational dispatches sent to the daily press throughout the country. Nothing could be more idiotic.[6]

Captain George McKay, John's brother, also stated publicly that he considered the entire incident a farce. He apparently never saw the bottled note however, and therefore could not firmly declare the signature invalid.

Like many around Lake Superior, George McKay was obviously very deeply saddened to hear of the MANISTEE'S loss. The brothers were both well-known skippers, and respected each other greatly. John A. Jacobs later recalled a visit he had with Captain George:

> I was in Cleveland later on and on invitation from Captain George McKay, a brother of Captain John, I called at his office. He questioned me closely about that night in Bayfield. He asked particularly how the boat was loaded; how the crew felt about going out, etc. He cried like a child and I thought he must have had a wonderful love for his brother.[7]

Persistent rumors concerning the MANISTEE'S "other" cargo abound, and warrant mention. On board there were allegedly 100 tons of pure copper bars, plus a large quantity of gold and silver in the ship's strongbox. The weight of the copper, some locals speculated, was obviously a factor in the MANISTEE'S list — if that is what happened. This "secret" cargo was never definitively proven.

The MANISTEE remains a ship of many mysteries. Somewhere, she sits at the bottom of Lake Superior, still holding her secrets to herself. The popular vessel was fittingly eulogized by the Bayfield newspaper:

> Probably the loss of no other boat that runs on this lake would have caused so much sorrow as has the loss of the MANISTEE. She seemed to belong to the people of those

towns, being the first boat to arrive in the spring and the last to leave in the fall. Her officers, and especially Capt. McKay, had the confidence and respect of all and were universal favorites with men, women and children.[8]

A sketch of the MANISTEE'S final minutes.

Larry W. Hoopman

Footnotes
1. BAYFIELD COUNTY PRESS, November 24, 1883.
2. Frederick Stonehouse in his book, **Went Missing,** presents some possible solutions to many of the MANISTEE riddles.
3. The terms "gross" and "net" tonnage are used throughout the book. The U.S. Department of Transportation defines them as: "The gross tonnage of a vessel is the internal cubic capacity of all space in and on the vessel which is permanently enclosed, with the exception of certain permissable exemptions. It is expressed in tons of 100 cubic feet."
"The net or register tonnage of a vessel is the remainder after deducting from the gross tonnage of the vessel the tonnage of crew spaces, master's accommodations, navigation spaces, allowance for propelling power, etc. It also is expressed in tons of 100 cubic feet."
4. **The Lake Superior Country in History and Story,** Guy Burnham, pg. 28.
5. DETROIT FREE PRESS, November 22, 1883.
6. ASHLAND NEWS, June 10, 1885.
7. **The Lake Superior Country in History and Story,** Guy Burnham, pg. 28.
8. BAYFIELD COUNTY PRESS, November 24, 1883.

OZAUKEE
A Bad River Battering

The little steamer OZAUKEE was a somewhat unique vessel. She was a sidewheel tug, 94 feet long and 17.5 feet wide. Used mainly to raft logs from Bad River to Ashland, the Union Mill Company worked her hard and often. In fact during the last couple years of her long life, local mariners apparently began to question her seaworthiness and many "considered her not very safe for some time."[1] A late May storm in 1884 tested the boat's questionable condition, and a day later the verdict was in. As the newspaper reported: "She lays away her bones to bleach on the shores of Getchee Gumme."[2]

The OZAUKEE was an old-timer on the lake, having seen many years of service. She was 66 gross tons (33 net), with a 6.2 foot depth. When she "died" she was owned by H.J. James of Ashland and, as mentioned, was used for towing rafts of logs into the Union Mill Company's sawmill. On May 26 she was performing a slightly different service but — perhaps fittingly — ended her career in a very familiar place.

It was mid-morning on Monday when the vessel left her Ashland dock. She was heading east, loaded down with supplies for south shore fishermen and Montreal River miners. With a stiff breeze blowing in her face, the OZAUKEE plodded on through the morning and into the afternoon. Under the circumstances she was making respectable time, but this situation was soon to change:

> Everything went well until about five o'clock in the evening, when the sea became very heavy as it had been blowing steadily from the northeast all day. When off Marble Point, she rolled so heavily that her steam whistle pipe broke, letting all the steam escape from her boiler, which left her to the mercy of the waves.[3]

The captain ordered the anchors dropped immediately, and — luckily — they held. Under the wild rocking of the boat, crewmembers began the laborious task of repairing the broken pipe. Sometime before nightfall the fishermen who were to receive part of OZAUKEE'S cargo, spotted the disabled vessel. They eventually decided to brave the high waves, and set out in their mackinaw boats for the steamer.[4] With great difficulty they managed to reach the tug, and began loading the freight into their mackinaws. The wind and waves were still moving strong, but they continued to make trips from the shore to the ship and back again. Throughout the night they worked, repeating the short but dangerous jaunt. By morning they had their fair share of freight, and the steam pipe was back in operable condition.

The fire in the boiler was rebuilt and the OZAUKEE, with full power, was back in business. The situation still had a grim side to it however: the bad weather was getting increasingly worse. The wind was "now a stiff gale, and the seas ran mountains high."[5] Deciding that an Ashland heading would be the wisest move, the captain ordered the anchors weighed.

The sidewheeler departed for her home port, but didn't make it far. The "mountain high" waves started to wash over the boat and she began to take on water. Knowing that there was no chance of making Ashland, the captain decided to run for the mouth of the Bad River. The pumps couldn't rid the hold of the inrushing seas however, and time was quickly running out. Finally, lowering the lifeboat and abandoning ship was all that could be done.

The lifeboat was launched and the entire crew safely made it to shore. The wild waves were not yet done with the OZAUKEE however. Battered and beaten, the boat was thrown up on the beach just 500 feet west of the Bad River's mouth. There she lay, being pounded to pieces by the cruel seas. Finally, much of her upper works were washed away.

That night with the riotous seas quieting, the crew managed to climb aboard the stranded steamer and salvage some cargo. Several days later the boiler and machinery were picked off. The owner endured a $3,000 uninsured loss, but must have remained optimistic. The following Saturday the newspaper reported:

> A new hull will be built for her machinery at once, in fact men are already at work getting out the necessary timber, and a new OZAUKEE will be afloat about the 1st of August.[6]

Footnotes
1. BAYFIELD COUNTY PRESS, May 31, 1884.
2. ASHLAND PRESS, May 31, 1884.
3. Ibid.
4. Mackinaw boats were small flat bottomed vessels formerly common in the upper Great Lakes area.
5. ASHLAND PRESS, May 31, 1884.
6. Ibid.

PRUSSIA
A Lightkeeper's Heroism

A Canadian vessel with a German name once paid an unscheduled — and permanent — call on Apostle Island waters. The steamer PRUSSIA met her fate on September 12th, 1885 near Sand Island. She was one more in a long line of ships which would sail their last here, and her tale — like many others — is one of danger, despair and heroics.

Built in 1874 the PRUSSIA was 458 tons burden. She was owned by Graham, Horn and Company of Port Arthur Ontario, and was operated by the Western Express Line.[1] The ship had sailed on all of the Great Lakes carrying a variety of cargo in her eleven year lifespan. She was crewed by ten men and one woman, and captained by William Anderson, an experienced lake Skipper.

On Friday, September 11th the PRUSSIA steamed away from her Port Arthur dock into a fresh southeast breeze. She was light, bound first for Duluth to pick up grain, then to distant Montreal to deliver it. Good progress was made the first few hours, but as darkness fell the wind and waves steadily increased. Captain Anderson decided to alter his course to port sometime during the night, hoping to gain the lee of the south shore. By morning's first light the southeast wind was blowing at close to gale force, and a heavy sea was running. The Apostles were in sight however, and Anderson elected to seek shelter there.

Sometime around 7:00 a.m., while heading for Sand Island, the Captain suddenly noticed flames springing up from the deck near the smokestack. The alarm was sounded immediately, but the fire, which had started under the boilers, had spread rapidly and was already quite intense. The crew desperately tried to fight the blaze but the fierce winds whipped the flames in every direction. Finally, ten miles from Sand Island, the decision was made to abandon the burning ship. The captain, first mate, engineer and fireman manned one lifeboat while the rest of the crew took to the second. As a newspaper account later reported "The fire spread with such rapidity that the crew in escaping lost most all of their effects,

35

Rare photo of the steamer PRUSSIA. C. Patrick Labadie Collection

some departing hatless and shoeless."[2]

The captain and men in the first boat bravely battled the battering seas, and made good headway toward Sand Island. The seven occupants of the other boat however, were losing their struggle. They desperately pulled at the oars, but were helplessly being blown out into the open lake. Their strongest efforts were proving futile against the mighty storm. The doomed seven watched hopelessly as land receded farther from view. It looked as if an angry Superior would claim not only the PRUSSIA, but also part of her crew.

It was a courageous man named Charles Lederlee, the Sand Island lighthouse keeper, who robbed Superior of her claim. From his vantage point in the tower he had seen the PRUSSIA burst into flame. Wasting no time he rushed down to his boat and shoved off. His small craft was pounded by the huge waves, but he stayed his course to the burning steamer. Several miles out he came upon the four men in the first lifeboat. They informed him that the ship had been abandoned, but the rest of the crew were in terrible trouble. Lederlee continued on through the storm until finally, he sighted the other lifeboat, still afloat with all occupants alive. The crew, who had already given up hope and simply surrendered their fate could not believe their eyes. Lederlee quickly picked them up and left the doomed lifeboat to the elements. On his way in, he picked up the other four and returned everybody safely to Sand Island and salvation.

Mr. Lederlee and his wife housed and fed the castaways until the storm abated the following day. He then brought the grateful crew to Bayfield. As for the PRUSSIA, her fate was sealed: she drifted a short way, burned to the waterline, and sank. The steamer was a total loss, but luckily was fully insured. The real "luck" of course, came in the form of a brave man who risked his own life to save the crew of the ill-fated PRUSSIA. The appreciation of those he rescued was sincerely expressed in a document they later presented to him:

SAND ISLAND, WIS., SEPT. 12, 1885.
TO THE LIGHTHOUSE KEEPER:

DEAR SIR: We, the undersigned crew of the propeller Prussia, feel it our duty to express our gratitude to you and your wife, as keeper of the Sand Island lighthouse, for kindness and assistance shown towards us while remaining at your house. We also wish to thank Mr. Lederlee for going to the rescue of the yawl boat and crew, as if he had not done so they would most likely have been lost, as there was a heavy sea running from the southeast and they were unable to pull up against it.

Signed in behalf of the officers and crew by
WM. ANDERSON, Capt.
SAMUEL BRISBIN, 1st Eng.
ISAAC EDWARD, 1st Mate [3]

Footnotes

1. Today Port Arthur is part of Thunder Bay.
2. BAYFIELD COUNTY PRESS, September 19th, 1885.
3. Ibid.

LUCERNE
Frozen Death

The year was 1886. The month was November. The unexpected tempest was "the heaviest northeaster experienced here for several years, accompanied by a blinding snowstorm that prevailed for upwards of forty-eight hours."[1] The casualty was the big schooner LUCERNE, which at the time was "considered one of the best on the freshwaters."[2]

On Sunday, November 14th the steam vessel RALEIGH arrived at Ashland with the LUCERNE in tow. The steamer's skipper, William Mack, was part owner of the LUCERNE and was known to have great confidence in her. The sleek and sturdy schooner was 728 gross tons and 195 feet long. She carried a crew of nine, captained by George S. Lloyd, and had a reputation for being fast. Having just received all new canvas, the LUCERNE was expected to make good time on her last run of the season.

The LUCERNE was loaded with 1200 tons of iron ore at Ashland on Monday. The cargo, 130 tons shy of her normal load, was consigned to Little, Oglebay and Company of Cleveland. That evening Captain Lloyd and crew set sail for their home port destination. With a light load, new canvas and a fair wind blowing, all the signs pointed to a speedy, successful voyage. Unfortunately, the expected outcome was never realized.

The November northeaster began stirring that night. As the LUCERNE cleared the shelter of Chequamegon Bay the wind picked up, but the decision to continue seemed a good one. After all, Lloyd was a well-seasoned skipper and the LUCERNE a veteran vessel. Both had previously proven themselves in heavy weather. They sailed on, hoping that morning light would find the storm diminishing.

Dawn grudgingly arrived, but without the desired results. A gale had erupted, the seas grew and the temperature dropped. A snowstorm now engulfed western Superior, and the LUCERNE found the going increasingly difficult. By afternoon the situation was critical: waves crashed over the vessel's deck while a furious wind clawed at the new canvas. The

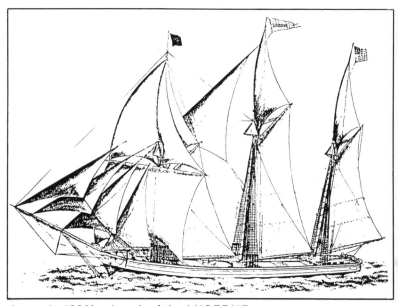

An early 1880's sketch of the LUCERNE.

LUCERNE was now caught up in combat with a snowy Superior hurricane, and simple survival would be declared victory.

At the height of the storm a steamer bound for Ashland passed the LUCERNE. The captain of the FRED KELLEY spotted the embattled schooner, but under the circumstances could offer no assistance. The LUCERNE, in sad shape by this time, was last seen turning tail and running for the lee of Long Island. The steamer's skipper later reported watching "the ill-fated schooner rolling and pitching about on the lake, evidently at the mercy of wind and waves."[3] Superior ultimately offered no mercy though, and the LUCERNE met a horrible end. Approaching the bay, the "wind and waves" finally devoured the battered boat.

No one witnessed the beaten boat's final minutes, and no one on board lived to tell the tale. In fact it wasn't until Friday of that week that the vessel's fate was discovered. William Mack, becoming worried about his LUCERNE, finally telegraphed Bayfield and asked that a tug be dispatched as a search vessel. The S.B. BARKER didn't have to go very far to find the LUCERNE'S final resting place. The crew discerned three masts sticking out of the water a short distance off of Long Island shore. Upon closer inspection the crew of the tug came upon a grisly sight. Aloft in the rigging they saw three of the ship's crewmembers — frozen solid. They had evidently climbed the masts to escape the freezing Superior seas, and there had perished waiting for help. Owing to still relatively high seas, the BARKER couldn't get any closer to the wreck, and turned back to port with the tragic news.

The following day the tug pushed out to the scene again, and the bodies were brought down by two Bayfield locals. The Bayfield County Press printed the following:

> Much credit is due Ed and Charlie Herbert for the work they did in ascending the masts of the wrecked schooner LUCERNE, and cutting down the bodies of the dead sailors lashed thereto. To do it required a good deal of skill and nerve, qualities the boys are not lacking in.[4]

The dead crewmembers were brought into Ashland, and laid in the undertaking rooms of Bicksler's Bazar. The Ashland newspaper dutifully reported that "The bodies were covered with from one to six inches of ice."[5]

Recovery teams searched the immediate area for days but came up with nothing. The newspaper reported the following interesting explanation:

> The balance of the shipmates still remain upon the wreck or have been swept out into the lake, which seldom ever gives up its dead...Of the sufferings of that crew there will never be a written account, but in the unwritten annals which go to make up the history of individuals, there

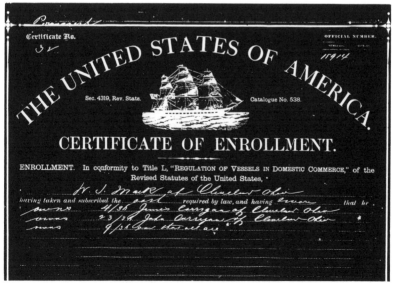

A section of the LUCERNE'S Certificate of Enrollment.

The FRED KELLEY sighted the LUCERNE at the height of the gale.

will undoubtedly be found tales of heroism and bravery in the meeting of deaths in the terrible manner which came to them. Those men went down to death, meeting it in a double manner...by drowning and freezing.[6]

The following year a partially decomposed body washed up on shore, and it was thought that he was another one of the LUCERNE'S crew.

The three dead sailors in Ashland were "embalmed by Henry Scott, who has preserved a wonderfully natural and lifelike appearance."[7] Nobody immediately identified or claimed any of the three however, and the Ashland newspaper ran the following descriptions:

One is heavily dressed, having on five coats besides heavy underwear. Feet were bare. Height 5 feet 10 inches; weight about 160 lbs. His age cannot be far from 45. Heavy sandy moustache, but no beard. One of the others wore a heavy sandy beard, was 5 feet 10 inches tall, and was about 40 years old. He was also heavily dressed, and had on rubber boots. The other was a young man, smooth face, 5 feet 9 inches tall, weight 135, and about 21 years old. He was scantily dressed, but wore high top boots. It is not deemed necessary to hold a coroners inquest, and unless some are found who claim the bodies they will be buried today (Saturday).[8]

The bodies were buried in the Ashland cemetery. Shortly thereafter, one man, Robert Jeffrey, was identified, dug up and claimed. Jeffrey was the son of Captain Robert J. Jeffrey, a famous old lake skipper. "It was his son's first trip on the

42

VESSEL LOST!

Schooner Lucern, of Cleveland, Loaded With Iron Ore, Sinks off Light House Point.

THE VESSEL GOES DOWN IN THREE FATHOMS OF WATER.

Crew of Nine Men Lost, Three of Whom are Found Lashed to the Rigging, and Brought to This City.

Headline in Ashland newspaper about LUCERNE.
Wisconsin State Historical Society

Bicksler's Bazar,

(ESTABLISHED 1873.)

FURNITURE,

---UNDERTAKING,---

And House Furnishing Goods,

PICTURE FRAMES, CHROMOS, ENGRAVINGS, TOYS, FANCY GOODS, NOTIONS,

Dry Goods, Ladies Furnishing Goods, Millinery, Trimmings, Wall Paper, Crockery, Glassware,

In fact, nearly everything that is useful, ornamental and serviceable in the family. Bicksler's Bazar is a distinct feature in the retail trade of Ashland. Motto, "Quick Sales and Small Profits." Terms cash.

Ashland Jan. 1, 1886   **B. F. BICKSLER.**

Advertisement for Bicksler's Bazar — besides undertaking rooms they had "nearly everything that is useful, ornamental and serviceable."
Wisconsin State Historical Society

43

LUCERNE and as it proved, his last earthly voyage."[9] The other two bodies were eventually identified, and shipped to their homes for proper burial.

The LUCERNE was a total loss, estimated to be worth $33,000. Like several before and many after, the magnificent schooner simply fell victim to the Superior heavy weather of November.

Death certificates for two of the LUCERNE'S crewmembers.

Canal Park Marine Museum

Footnotes

1. BAYFIELD COUNTY PRESS, Nov. 20, 1886.
2. ASHLAND PRESS, Nov. 20, 1886.
3. Ibid.
4. BAYFIELD COUNTY PRESS, Nov. 27, 1886.
5. ASHLAND PRESS, Nov. 20, 1886.
6. Ibid.
7. ASHLAND NEWS, Dec. 1, 1886.
8. ASHLAND PRESS, Nov. 20, 1886.
9. ASHLAND DAILY PRESS, Nov. 27, 1886.

CITY OF ASHLAND
The Namesake Ship

Anxiety and fear ran high along the shores of Chequamegon Bay one windy Monday in 1887. Hundreds of people lined the waters edge while the tug CITY OF ASHLAND was being eaten by flames in plain sight out on the bay. Rumors flew among the crowds, the most persistent being that all crewmembers had perished in the blaze. Five steamers and tugs had rushed to the rescue, but the huge fire definitively told the story of the ASHLAND'S fate. She was fast becoming a memory to the city from which she took her name.

On the afternoon of August 8th the CITY OF ASHLAND was carrying out her normal duty of towing a raft of logs into her namesake city. The staunch little steamer was owned by the Superior Lumber Company of Ashland, and was a familiar sight on the bay. As throngs of trees were being felled in and around Bad River they'd multiply near the shore where the ASHLAND would pick them up and tow them in rafts to the sawmill. Captain Barney Doherty was at the helm, having taken over only ten days prior to the fire. Under Doherty was a crew of five who worked the tug.

A heavy wind was kicking up high seas that ill-fated Monday, but the ASHLAND had little trouble bringing her raft from Bad River. She had rounded Chequamegon Point and was on the "home stretch" to the sawmill. Suddenly, at a point just three miles northeast of Washburn, fire was discovered at the rear of the pilot house. It was only minutes before the entire boat was enveloped in flames. The crew could do nothing but attempt to save themselves. The old ASHLAND NEWS reported: "In a moment the vessel was all aflame and as the wind was blowing very strong it gave no time for those on board to save anything, and indeed they barely escaped with their lives, even before leaping into the water."[1]

Jumping into Superior's chilly seas with high waves was a far cry from certain salvation, but abandoning the burning hulk was the only option open. Captain Doherty was the last man off the boat, leaving after the rest of the crew had safely taken the plunge. Swimming away from the incredibly intense heat,

A BAY STEAMER BURNED

The Tug City of Ashland Burned to the Water's Edge on Monday.

Fred. Ebert, One of the Firemen, Drowned while Attempting to Escape.

Peculiarly Daring Robbery at Mrs. Bicksler's Millinery Store on Saturday.

A SAD FATALITY.

Ashland Newspaper headline reporting the loss of the steamer CITY OF ASHLAND. Wisconsin State Historical Society

most of the crew quickly found logs to hang onto. "The engineer and fireman floated and swam back to the raft, which was 1000 feet in the rear. Three more of the crew floated in the water...grasping a few slabs to support themselves."[2] The CITY OF ASHLAND actually carried eighteen life preservers, but in the terrible excitement with the fire spreading so rapidly, none were grabbed!

Two tugs immediately set out to help the imperiled crew. It was over a half an hour before they arrived however, and this was too long a wait for one man. A fireman, Fred Ebert, did not

The S.B. BARKER at Devils Island. She rescued two crewmembers from the CITY OF ASHLAND.

know at all how to swim, and the big waves eventually got the best of him. A brave Captain Doherty attempted to rescue the struggling crewmember, but his efforts were in vain. "He did all in his power to save the life of Fred Ebert by encouraging him and telling him to hold onto his slab, but he let go of it, and sank before the captain could reach him...The poor fellow met his watery grave."[3] Another man, Peter Sturgeon, might have been added to the fatality list, but Doherty swam over to him, offered encouragement and physically helped him hang on for dear life.

The tugs CYCLONE and S.B. BARKER were the first two boats on the scene, and immediately began saving the exhausted survivors. The CYCLONE went first to the raft and picked up the engineer and fireman, then grabbed a third crewmember floating on a slab. The BARKER meanwhile rushed to the fading Peter Sturgeon and dragged him aboard just in time. Finally a rope was thrown to Captain Doherty, who

47

by this time had been in the cold water for forty five minutes, and he was hauled safely aboard the BARKER. Three other vessels had arrived by this time, but could do little except watch the CITY OF ASHLAND flame and finally founder. The newspaper reported the condition of the men: "All of those taken from the water were much benumbed and prostrated from their long continuance in the cold water. As the wind was blowing hard and the waves running high it rendered their situation a very critical one."[4]

The origin of the fire remained an unsolved riddle, but it had consumed virtually everything before the boat sank. Captain Doherty estimated the loss at approximately $8000, with only $2500 insurance coverage on it. The log raft was salvaged, but the boat and one crewmember would sail no more. The CITY OF ASHLAND still lies at the bottom of the bay, close to her namesake city.

Footnotes

1. ASHLAND NEWS, August 10, 1887.
2. Ibid.
3. ibid.
4. Ibid.

MARY CARGAN
Victim of Impatience?!

In September of 1887, one month after the CITY OF ASHLAND burned in Chequamegon Bay, the Superior Lumber Company bought another vessel to replace her. The MARY CARGAN was her name, and like the ill-fated ASHLAND she too eventually found her way to the bottom of Lake Superior.[1] On a storm-driven day in December of 1891 the CARGAN arrived at her final resting place near Sand Island. By ominous coincidence she was being towed by the T.H. CAMP, a future bottom dweller herself, when she went down.

The MARY CARGAN was a small but sturdy steamer of approximately 75 tons. She was captained by Barney Doherty, previously the skipper of the CITY OF ASHLAND, and engineered by Bower Lewis. Like her predecessor,the CARGAN was used to raft logs from Bad River to the Superior Company's sawmill in Ashland. This proved to be a short term occupation for the little boat however. In 1888 she was sold to the Booth Packing Company of Bayfield and "was engaged in the fish business at that place and Washburn for several years."[2] The CARGAN carried out her duties for the Booth Company through the 1891 season, and then was sold to some Duluth businessmen. In December of that year she was headed to her new home port and owners, but she never made it...

The tug T.H. CAMP picked up the MARY CARGAN at Bayfield and departed the evening of December 7th. They would presumably make Duluth sometime early in the morning if all went well. There was a fairly strong wind blowing when they left port, but initially the islands would offer protection. The crew knew that these late season voyages were always potentially dangerous because of Superior's volatile temperament that time of year. The new owners, however, evidently wanted their boat before winter called a halt to shipping. Perhaps this impatience was the reason that they never did take possession of the CARGAN.

With the CARGAN in tow the T.H. CAMP steamed up the West Channel and began rounding the peninsula. The gale by this time was increasing in severity, but the tug stayed in the

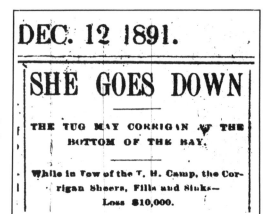

lee of Oak, Raspberry and York Islands. Approaching Sand Island the waves grew larger and the two boats were having difficulty making headway. This problem was intensified by the fact that, inexplicably, there was nobody on board the CARGAN to steer her! With each pounding wave she'd deviate from the desired course, producing dire problems for the CAMP. With the CARGAN being pushed about at will, the strain on the towline finally became too great and it snapped.

The T.H. CAMP immediately turned around to try and rescue its drifting consort. With nobody on board to guide the little CARGAN however, the waves began pounding over her. She endured no more than a few minutes, and, as the newspaper reported, "The wind and waves sheered the boat, it quickly filled, and sank."[3] There was nothing for the crewmembers of the CAMP to do now but steam back to Bayfield and report the loss.

The CARGAN sank in relatively shallow water, estimated at the time to be only 30 feet. Consequently there was serious talk of salvaging her, but, as the papers reported "She cannot be raised until sufficiently fine weather to enable the undertaking."[4] Evidently "sufficient" weather never came. The long north country winter arrived shortly after, and the idea — along with the boat — was simply abandoned. The loss to the Duluth owners: $10,000. The purchase of the MARY CARGAN certainly did not prove to be a successful business venture!

Footnotes

1. Several different names appeared in various newspapers (MAY CARGAN MAR CORRIGAN), but MARY CARGAN is most likely the correct one.
2. ASHLAND DAILY PRESS, December 8th, 1891.
3. Ibid.
4. BAYFIELD COUNTY PRESS, December 12, 1891.

M.R. WARNER
Slowly...But Surely

For Lake Superior sailors November has traditionally been the most vicious month of the year. Blinding snow, wicked winds and awesome waves have often combined to tear many a good ship to shreds. The devastating gales that plague these late season seas have become legend. The infamous November northeasters were flexing their muscles again in 1893, but not in one great show of strength. This time it was spread over a long period, with a constancy that finally wore down its victim. The casualty was the twenty year old schooner M.R. WARNER.

The M.R. WARNER was a good sized sailing vessel when she was launched in 1873. She was a wooden three-master built in Toledo, Ohio, by the J.E. Baily shipbuilders. The ship measured 199.3 feet in length, 34.3 feet in beam, 14.4 feet in depth, and was 699.95 gross tons (644.95 net). She was built for Shepard, Henry and Company of Erie, Pennsylvania to be used as a consort for the bulk steamer FRED KELLEY.[1] Both ships were used for the iron ore trade between Escanaba, Michigan and Cleveland, with the schooner's cargo capacity being approximately 1500 tons. The WARNER was later sold to Palmer, Johnson and Company of Cleveland, who were engaged in the iron ore and grain trades. They in turn sold her to the Bradley Lumber fleet of Cleveland who were the ship's final owners.

On Wednesday, November 1st, 1893 the M.R. WARNER departed Duluth, downbound for Tonawanda, New York. She sailed out into a northeast breeze, heavily laden with a cargo of lumber. Out of port the schooner evidently found the going rather difficult. After two days had passed, with the WARNER'S whereabouts completely unknown, the owners became worried. On November 4th the Ashland Daily Press reported: "No trace of schooner WARNER, although a strict search is being made; the worst is feared."[2&3]

The search proved successful — the M.R. WARNER was discovered to be aground on the west side of Sand Island. For two full days the big vessel had plowed on, making very little headway against the wind and waves. On Friday the captain

The BESSIE SMITH, MARY JARECKI and M.R. WARNER (far right) caught in an ice field.

evidently decided to seek shelter in the lee of Sand Island, and the ship was blown ashore. When the schooner was found she was in decidedly bad shape. "Half of her deckload of lumber has gone, her starboard quarter is gone, and she is broken amidships. The first big wind will blow her to pieces."[4] Luckily the crew were all safe and sound, and were eventually taken back to Duluth.

Salvage efforts were immediately begun. The weather calmed, and the tugs SMITH and SAMPSON went to the ship's aid. Apparently it was felt that the WARNER had a good chance of being saved — if the weather continued to cooperate. Relying on good weather on Lake Superior in November, however, is never a safe bet.

The eleventh month of 1893, as usual, did not produce the desired weather. The wind and waves kept beating on the stranded schooner, and bit by bit she was breaking up. The vessels sent to free the M.R. WARNER did what they could, but with the boat still stuck and time running out, their efforts were largely in vain. Notorious November did not offer them much of a chance to get any work done. Finally the decision to abandon the operation became inevitable, and Lake Superior scored another. The Port Huron Daily Times on November 29th related: "schooner WARNER, ashore at Sand Island, has broken up. Only 250,000 feet of lumber was saved by the wrecking outfit which was there for two weeks, and had only two and a half days of calm waters to work on her."[5]

The M.R. WARNER had fallen prey to Lake Superior's late season tantrums. On this occasion it was not one great herculean blow however, as is often the case. The great lake simply wore down its victim, in a sort of war of attrition. With a constant wind and a pounding wave, the M.R. WARNER finally surrendered to Superior.

Footnotes

1. The FRED KELLEY was the vessel that had reported seeing the LUCERNE shortly before she foundered in 1886.

2. ASHLAND DAILY PRESS, November 4, 1893.

3. Some newspapers reported that the WARNER was under tow of another Bradley boat, the CITY OF SUPERIOR, but this possibility seems unlikely. If that had been the case, the steamer presumably would have gone to the nearest port and reported the accident, which never happened. The WARNER'S plight was discovered only after local vessels had searched for two days.

4. DULUTH NEWS TRIBUNE, November 5, 1893.

5. PORT HURON DAILY TIMES, November 29, 1893.

ANTELOPE
A Name With A Curse

Our deck was coated with tons of ice,
But not a sailor knew,
Some would be froze and some be drowned
Of our big freighter's crew.

The huge seas raked her fore and aft,
The cold wind loud did roar,
We struck stern on and swung broadside
To our doom on Superior.

Lake Song, 1894

The Lake song was a well known and oft-repeated ballad on the Great Lakes. It originally celebrated the loss of a vessel named the ANTELOPE. This particular name was quite popular with ship-owners in the late 1800's. At one time just prior to the turn of the century there were no less than thirteen ANTELOPES plying the inland seas: seven schooners, two propellors, one brig, one scow, one barge and one tug. It was a popular title, but one which also seemed to openly invite cruel fate in the form of death and destruction. All the ANTELOPES of that period at one time or another suffered terrible luck by capsizing, foundering, stranding or burning. Ships bearing that ill-fated name were lost all over the Great Lakes!

The water of the Apostles had to lay claim to its ANTELOPE of course, and this it did in 1897. The ship was owned by L.S. Bowtell of Bay City, Michigan, and was ending her days traversing the lakes as a tow barge. The vessel had endured a peculiar career, being somewhat of an anomaly in Great Lakes shipping history. She was originally one of the early steamships on the lakes, but was later converted to a scooner. Built in 1861 in Newport, Michigan she initially carried passengers between Buffalo and Chicago. Some years later her duties became more cargo oriented, and converting her to a schooner meant more freight carrying space. Even as a sailing ship though she still carried her stack right to the end.

On the morning of October 7th, 1897 the steamer HIRAM W.

The converted steamer ANTELOPE.

University of Detroit Marine Historical Collection.

SIBLEY was towing the ANTELOPE, both vessels heavily laden with coal from ports on the lower lakes. The ANTELOPE with her cargo was to be dropped off at the Pennsylvania and Ashland Coal Company dock in Ashland, while the SIBLEY would continue west to unload at Duluth. Approaching Michigan Island the ANTELOPE suddenly started to leak. The crew immediately put the pumps to work and tried to locate the problem. The pumps could not cope with the inrushing sea however, and the level of water in the hold steadily and rapidly rose. The men did all they could to save the ship, but it soon became apparent that the ANTELOPE was doomed. The men quickly gathered up their personal possessions, the vessel's documents and other articles of value that could be easily moved, and prepared to board the SIBLEY. All crewmembers were safely transferred and the towline was parted. Within minutes the ANTELOPE, like so many of her namesakes, was resting at the bottom of the sea.

The captain of the SIBLEY then elected to bypass Ashland and sail straight to Duluth. The ship and crew arrived at port at

The ANTELOPE dry-docked at the Davidson yards, West Bay City, Michigan.
Ralph K. Roberts collection

8:00 that night with the news of the lost vessel. The reason given for the ANTELOPE'S foundering was that her seams simply opened up. The schooner's old timbers could not withstand the combined effects of a twelve mile per hour tow and the choppy seas that prevailed that day. She was 187 feet long, 34 feet wide, 12 feet deep and 523 tons burden. The loss including the cargo was estimated at $35,000.

The ANTELOPE of the Apostles was one of the more famous ships bearing that name. At one time she was a highly respected vessel and quite a familiar sight on the lakes. Upon her "death", the Duluth News Tribune printed a rather fitting eulogy: "Twenty five or thirty years ago she was one of the cracker-jacks, a thing of beauty and an object of pride. In those days the ANTELOPE was well-known and much admired..."[1]

Footnote
1. DULUTH NEWS TRIBUNE, October 8th, 1897.

R.G. STEWART
A Packet Steamer Peril

Captain Cornelius "Con" Flynn was carrying on a long and interesting Great Lakes tradition in 1899. He owned and personally skippered a small packet steamer which he operated along the south shore of Lake Superior. The packet steamers — successors of the small "coaster" sailing vessels — would carry passengers and a diversity of cargo to various ports, small and large. Flynn had been running the R.G. STEWART along his regular south shore route for several seasons, and did a very profitable business. The STEWART was a staunch little craft and had given the captain few problems over the years. In a thick fog in June of 1899 however, the ship unexpectedly met one of the Apostles, and Flynn's business met an abrupt end.

On Saturday, June 3rd Captain Flynn left Hancock, Michigan with three passengers and sort of an unusual cargo: cattle. Their destination was Flynn's home port of Duluth. Shortly after leaving Ontonogan, their only scheduled stop, a heavy fog descended upon the already black night, and visibility became virtually nonexistent. At 11:00 p.m., running blind, the R.G. STEWART suddenly crashed aground on Michigan Island. All efforts to free her failed, and the crew and passengers resigned themselves to a night in the Apostles. The lake was relatively calm so there was no danger, and they felt the problem could be more easily dealt with the following day.

Sunday morning dawned and the crew scanned the waters for a passing vessel which could hopefully offer help. No ships were sighted however, and Captain Flynn decided to deal with the problem himself. The engines were started and he pushed them feverishly in hopes of backing the STEWART off her stranding point. Flynn tried time and again until suddenly, fire was discovered below deck. The boilers had overheated in the effort to free the ship, and the engine room was ablaze. Before long the little steamer was a mass of flames. The men tried everything to fight the fire, but to no avail. Everybody gathered up what possessions they could and the cattle were pushed

The Packet steamer R.G. STEWART with passengers posing nicely.

The R.G. STEWART again loaded with passengers.

overboard. The lifeboat had already been launched and tied up alongside the STEWART, and people began boarding. First the passengers climbed in followed by the captain and seven crewmembers. Wheelsman George McKenna was to cast off the line and then board the lifeboat, but the flames evidently were getting too close for comfort. McKenna panicked and jumped from the STEWART'S deck on to the gunwale of the lifeboat, completely capsizing it and sending everyone into Superior's frigid seas! As the newspaper later commented. "It was then every man for himself!"[1]

Six men including McKenna tried to swim to the nearby shore, while the other six clung to the overturned lifeboat. The terrified McKenna couldn't make it though, and slipped beneath the surface. A crewmember immediately swam over to him, pulled him and tried desperately to revive him. The gallant effort was unsuccessful however — Wheelsman McKenna was dead.

The remaining five men made it safely to shore, while the other six successfully managed to right the lifeboat and climb in. One problem remained. In his fright, McKenna never did cast the lifeboat's line off! She was still tied tight to the flaming hull that was once the R.G. STEWART. The ship's boat carried no axe and nobody on board had a knife on them. The six men, in fact, couldn't even get near the hawser because of the incredibly intense heat. Finally the line burned through and the lifeboat was set adrift. The men, much hotter for their experience, were nonetheless soon safe and sound on shore.

Everything was lost except for what the men were wearing. Along with his boat and personal possessions, Captain Flynn lost $300 in silver. He later claimed that he was very happy not to be wearing the trousers which contained the silver, for if he had "the weight would have surely drowned him."[2] The eleven survivors were found by the keeper of the Michigan Island lighthouse, who offered them food, shelter and lodging for the night. The following morning he took the stranded men and McKenna's body to Bayfield in his boat. The men finally made it to Duluth aboard the steamship HUNTER. McKenna's body was shipped to his home of Detroit for burial.

The R.G. STEWART was built in Buffalo in 1878 and used originally as a ferry on the Niagara River. She was brought to Duluth in 1882 and bought by Captain Flynn in 1894. The steamer was 100 feet long, 23 feet wide, with a gross tonnage of 197. She was a total loss estimated at $10,000, but insured for only $6000. The remains of the STEWART still lie in shallow water off Michigan Island. Interesting to note is the fact that the entire uninsured cargo was saved: all the cattle swam to shore.

Footnotes
1. ASHLAND NEWS June 6, 1899.
2. ASHLAND DAILY PRESS June 6, 1899.

SECTION II

Post 1900 Shipwrecks

T.H. CAMP
A Twenty Ton List
FEDORA
Full Speed Ahead
MOONLIGHT
A Legendary Schooner
MARQUETTE
Insured!
NOQUE BAY
A Stockton Blaze
SEVONA
Courage and Death
PRETORIA
One of the Largest
IRA H. OWEN
Went Missing
OTTAWA
The Famous Reid Wrecker
HERRING KING
Small Boat Tragedy
ONTARIO
The Prohibition Wreck

Post 1900 Era

The Chequamegon region continued to flourish economically in the early 1900's. The boom basically persisted until the Great Depression shut down many of the businesses. Cargo and vessels moved in and out of the area at a consistent rate during the first quarter of the century.

Ashland was a major shipping and railroading center throughout this period. At one time it sported over twenty sawmills, four coal docks and four oredocks — the last one built being "the most modern oredock in the world." Washburn was a booming little town in its own right — possessing three sawmills, a coal dock and a commercial dock. Bayfield enjoyed economic prosperity, relying mainly on its time-honored tradition of fishing.

The tonnage of cargo moved in the region increased every year. Commercial exports for the most part were lumber and iron ore. The brownstone business died out as quickly as it began, due to more modern building methods and materials. Coal continued to be shipped in in growing quantities.

The 1900's saw a great change in the types of vessels being

The Edward Hines Lumber fleet in Ashland harbor.

Ashland Historical Society

used. Tugs and fishing boats obviously abounded, but gone were the sidewheelers and the sailing vessels for the most part. Wooden bulk freighters and large steel steamers were being used almost exclusively now. The once proud schooners now found themselves being cut down into barges and ingloriously towed behind the smoke belching steamers. As the century progressed, the expanding network of railroads was replacing the packet steamer and her duties. Excursion boats, ferries and private yachts still plied the bay waters in great numbers.

A vital shipping center had developed at Chequamegon Bay. Growth was still the catchword and commerce the key. For sixty years the region enjoyed economic prosperity. This all ended of course in 1929 when Wall Street crashed. What was lost during the Depression was never fully regained. Never again would Chequamegon Bay hold a prominent position in Lake Superior shipping.

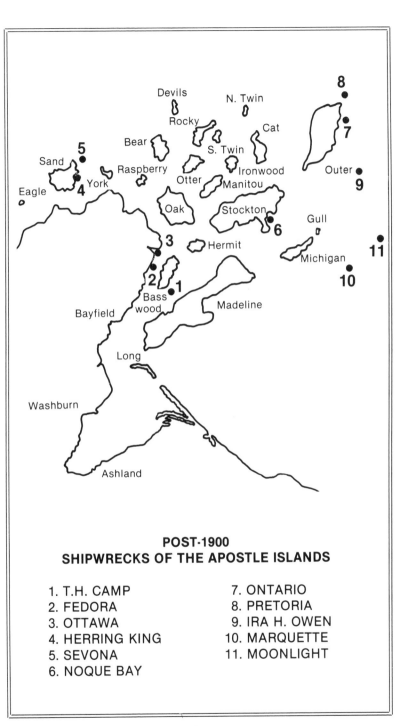

POST-1900
SHIPWRECKS OF THE APOSTLE ISLANDS

1. T.H. CAMP
2. FEDORA
3. OTTAWA
4. HERRING KING
5. SEVONA
6. NOQUE BAY

7. ONTARIO
8. PRETORIA
9. IRA H. OWEN
10. MARQUETTE
11. MOONLIGHT

T.H. CAMP
A Twenty Ton List

The first boat to find bottom in the Apostle Islands in the twentieth century was a tug named the T.H. CAMP. Owned by the Booth Packing Company of Bayfield, the tough little tug had become a mainstay of the local fleet. The well-known boat was quite a fixture on the bay, but all too soon became a fixture on the bottom. In November of 1900 with rough seas running and a cumbersome load on deck, the CAMP unfortunately settled into her deathbed. On a sandy bottom between Madeline and Basswood Islands the T.H. CAMP lay 180 feet below Superior's surface.

The wooden tug was a genuine old-timer, having been built in 1876 at Cape Vincent, New York. Her measurements were 64½ feet in length, 28 feet in beam, 5 feet in depth, and 58 gross tons. Through the years the T.H. CAMP had been involved in both rescues and wrecks — the latter notably being the MARY CARGAN Sand Island accident of 1891. Captain Swanson of Bayfield had been the CAMP'S skipper for years, carrying with him a three man crew.

At 1:30 in the afternoon on November 16th the T.H. CAMP began her final voyage. The little tug steamed out of Ashland loaded down with a cargo of camp supplies. She made a brief stop in Bayfield, apparently adding to her already heavily laden deck, and at 3:00 set out again. Her intended destination was the northern end of Madeline Island and the Brigham and Gardner logging camp. Unfortunately, the CAMP'S destiny lay no more than a few miles out of Bayfield.

The seas were a bit choppy that day, driven by a stiff northeast breeze, but the CAMP, as it had often done before, simply rolled with the punches. Heading into the North Channel between Basswood and Madeline the CAMP'S crew spied a sailboat that looked like it could use some assistance. At a point nearly opposite the brownstone quarry on Basswood Island, Captain Swanson ordered the engines put in reverse, with the intention of giving the sailboat a tow. Suddenly, the boat shivered a bit, and listed slightly to one side. The crew thought nothing of it though, knowing that the sturdy CAMP

A rare photograph of the T.H. CAMP.   Bayfield Heritage Association

could hold her own against these waves. Then, unexpectedly, the boat gave another lurch and listed a good three feet farther down than before. The crew was now deservedly alarmed: the tug was precariously perched with the waves splashing over the gunwale!

It was now evident to the captain what had happened: a large portion of the cargo had shifted. Swanson later recalled:

> *I supposed we had about twelve tons on, but now I think it was nearer twenty tons, and as it was all on deck, it made the boat top heavy. I thought of measuring the lifeboat, as I did not like the way she acted, but did not. We stopped and were backing up when the cargo listed.[1]*

With the CAMP now leaning dangerously to one side, water began pouring into the hold. It was plainly and painfully clear to the crew what was soon to happen — the T.H. CAMP had only a few minutes left!

An Ashland man, Dan Cronk, immediately tried to launch the metallic lifeboat, but this proved to be no easy task under the circumstances. The situation was growing increasingly desperate — when luck suddenly smiled upon them:

> *About this time the sailboat came up alongside, and the T.H. CAMP crew clambered on board, — just in time, for the CAMP immediately settled, then sank stern first in thirty fathoms of water. Dan Cronk was in the chilly waters up to his waist, but had a firm hold on a sailboat line, and managed to pull himself on board. It was a nar-*

VOL. 12   NO. 218

TUG CAMP SUNK

WENT DOWN IN THIRTY FATHOMS

All of the Crew Rescued By a Sail boat—A Cargo of Freight Lost With the Boat.

Ashland newspaper headline regarding T.H. CAMP'S loss.

row escape for the crew, and it seemed providential that the sailboat happened to be near at hand.[2]

The sailboat, along with its newly-acquired four man crew, put back to Bayfield. The CAMP'S survivors, as listed in the newspaper were: "Captain Swanson, Engineer McNeil and the fireman, all of Bayfield, and Dan Cronk of Ashland, who is engineer of the PLOWBOY during the summer season."[3&4] The only reminder of the T.H. CAMP that the men could salvage was the lifeboat, which they picked up floating on the surface.

Upon returning to Bayfield the crew reported the accident to the Booth Company offices. The T.H. CAMP was valued at approximately $5000, and the loss of cargo was simply listed as "considerable." Regarding the lost freight, there seemed to have been a dispute over whose responsibility it was, and who would pay for it. Because the CAMP was alleged to have been grossly overloaded, the Brigham and Gardner people felt it was a case of negligence on Booth Packing's part. Booth, in turn, claimed that they were running a risk in bringing such a large order. The final decision of where responsibility lay is not known.

Regardless of the argument's outcome, there is still twenty tons of logging camp supplies at the bottom of the North Channel. Because of the great depth and cold temperature of the water, the cargo is still mostly likely in relatively good shape. And somewhere amidst the many many tons of supplies lay the sturdy little tug T.H. CAMP — the first Apostle Island shipwreck in the twentieth century.

Footnotes
1. ASHLAND DAILY PRESS, November 19, 1900.
2. ASHLAND DAILY PRESS, November 17, 1900.
3. Ibid.
4. The PLOWBOY was a well-known ferry which made regular runs between Ashland, Washburn, Bayfield and LaPoint for many seasons.

THE FEDORA
Full Speed Ahead

The steamer FEDORA was built in West Bay City, Michigan in 1889. The ship's name was taken from a very popular play of that year which starred the famous stage actress Fanny Davenport. Miss Davenport was even present at the FEDORA'S launching and actually took the honor of christening her. This event of course received much public attention, and the original owner, E.D. Carter of Erie, Pennsylvania, could only hope this to be a good omen for his new vessel.

The FEDORA'S "specs" were impressive. She was 282.2 feet long, 41.5 feet wide, 20.1 feet deep and listed a gross tonnage of 1,848 — certainly a respectable size ship for her day. The vessel was of composite construction with keel, ribs and frame made of iron, but all plankings being oak. The FEDORA was considered one of the best of that style ever built. The marine insurance companies even classified her as among the safest ships on all the Great Lakes. The experienced and respected shipmaster Captain Frank A. Fick took over her helm in 1891, and was known to have great confidence in the vessel.[1]

On a windy cold September night in 1901 the FEDORA was making her way through the Apostle Islands. She was enroute to Ashland, having left the familar port of Duluth that afternoon. The FEDORA was said to have carried more grain out of Duluth than any other ship in her day, but on this particular trip her hold was empty. She was to pick up a load of iron ore at the Ashland docks and then head down to the lower lakes. The lights of her destination were just coming in view.

Since it was Friday night the crew of seventeen along with two passengers were looking forward to a short shore leave if time would permit. The short trip from Duluth had been rather uneventful, and a downbound voyage meant some long days on the water. As it turned out everybody was going to reach shore that night, but not at all under the circumstances they envisioned.

The FEDORA was in the West Channel just passing

The bulk freighter FEDORA

Basswood Island when suddenly a freak accident occurred. A kerosene lamp in the engine room exploded showering its deadly contents over everything. Before the engineer had time to react, flames sprang up throughout the room and he was forced to evacuate — with the steamer still running at full throttle! The fire spread with incredible speed and though the crew tried desperately to extinguish the blaze, their efforts proved futile. The entire ship was a mass of smoke and flames in minutes. Captain Fick immediately headed toward shore in hopes of beaching her before everybody was forced to abandon ship. The flaming FEDORA, steaming full speed ahead, ran hard aground with tremendous force just in time! All on board quickly climbed into the lowered lifeboats and frantically paddled the short way to shore and safety. It was a very narrow escape, but no one was seriously hurt.

Captain Fick later explained:

> The pumps which are utilised in case of fire are all in the engine room and in the same apartment where the large oil cans are stored. When the lamp exploded the oil in the cans was ignited, and before we could get anywhere near the pumps, the entire hold was inflamed. A strong southeast wind was raging at the time and fanned the flames into furious fiery tongues which, running high into the air illuminated the lake for a great distance and showed us a place of vantage to beach our sinking ship.[2]

The huge steamer burned on throughout the night, while Captain Fick and the exhausted crew watched helplessly. Their ship and personal possessions on board were going up in flames before their eyes, but they had come away with their lives. They shivered on shore through the long night, and at daybreak rowed the lifeboats to Bayfield. The OMAHA SCOTT then took them to Ashland, their original destination.

The FEDORA, unlike many boats of her day, was fully insured by her owner W.W. Brown of Cleveland. She was valued at $85,000 and insured for exactly that amount. The vessel was a complete loss. In fact, as the newspapers reported the following day, there were very few wrecks on the Great Lakes where so little of value remained. It seems that Captain Fick had so much confidence in his ship that he carried almost all of his personal belongings on board, estimated at several thousand dollars worth. Almost everything he owned burned with the ship.

As was often the case in those days, the wreck attracted many visitors immediately afterward. Tugs, fishing boats and private yachts loaded with people made excursions to see the remnants of the once proud ship. As the Ashland Daily Press reported "... The fire consumed everything of wood above the water line, and her frame remains a twisted and contorted mass of ribbons and beams, a most gruesome sight indeed!"[3]

Footnotes
1. Captain Fick claimed the honor of having taken the very first load of iron ore out of Ashland on July 13, 1884 when he was master of another vessel.
2. ASHLAND NEWS, September 21, 1901.
3. ASHLAND DAILY PRESS, September 23, 1901.

MOONLIGHT
A Legendary Schooner

The great era of sail on the unsalted seas took place in the mid to late nineteenth century. At one time there were almost 2000 cargo carrying sailing vessels plying the Great Lakes. Sailing the tall ships was undoubtedly tough, physical work, but a certain element of romance undeniably lent itself to those bygone days. Even the names of the vessels — STARLIGHT, DAWN, AURORA, GOLDEN FLEECE, MORNING STAR — inspired a certain romantic atmosphere. One of the fastest and most graceful boats of that period was a famous schooner appropriately called MOONLIGHT. Eventually she, like so many other proud sailing ships, outlived her era and was fitted out as a towbarge. At the end of her career she was being pulled by a smoke-belching steamer, going down in 1903. Her demise could be called "untimely," but perhaps only because it came too late.

The MOONLIGHT first touched water in Milwaukee harbor in 1874. She was built for William Mack of Cleveland, at the shipyards of the Wolf and Davidson Company.[1] The vessel was one of the larger class of freight carriers in her day: 777 gross tons (738 net), 206 feet long and 35 feet wide. Beauty, quickness, an innovative design and a hard driving skipper were the ingredients which made the MOONLIGHT both famous and fast.

Embodying the shipbuilding theories of the early 1870's the MOONLIGHT was distinctively designed. She was a three-master, her rigging consisting of fore and aft sails on the mizzen and mainmast, and a squaresail on the foremast. But unlike the traditional barkentine rig, she carried a large, billowing triangular topsail above the squaresail, known as a raffee. This rigging, of Great Lakes origin, was a compromise between the pure schooner carrying only fore and aft sails, and the barkentine with only squaresails on her foremast. This style of rigging was fairly common in the closing years of the sailing ship era on the Great Lakes.[2]

As the American clipper ships were making history on the high seas, the Great Lakes cargo vessels were beginning to

A painting of the legendary MOONLIGHT in moonlit waters

The MOONLIGHT under sail.
C. Patrick Labadie collection

carve out a piece of history for themselves. The "lakers," as they were often called, were a bit different from their ocean-going brethren.[3] Besides the compromise "raffee" rig lake schooners were usually longer and narrower than ocean vessels of similar tonnage. This design facilitated the use of narrow harbor entrances, canals and shallow ports found on the lakes. They also had flat sided hulls and used a center-board for sailing stability. The bigger vessels almost always carried three masts, but even they were somewhat different than the "salts." On the ocean schooners the masts were always the same height, approximately 91 to 93 feet. On a laker, typically, the mainmast was the tallest, up to about 103 feet, with the foremast somewhere around 98 feet, and the mizzen often dropping to 86 feet. This provided the lakers with a distinctive, graceful silhouetted form. They were fast, functional, and when a wind filled all canvas, these lakers were pure harmony of movement.

Only a few short years after she was built, the MOONLIGHT was generally acknowledged to be one of the finest — and fastest — cargo vessels on the Great Lakes. Her speed seemed to be a direct result of a workable combination: fine design, and a skipper named Dennis Sullivan who liked to

The MOONLIGHT aground near Marquette in 1896.

carry lots of sail. Impromptu races were often held between ships in those days, but one of the most famous Great Lakes races involved the MOONLIGHT. Captain Sullivan challenged Orv Green, captain of another notably fast schooner the PORTER, to some long distance competition. Both vessels happened to be leaving Buffalo at the same time, bound for Milwaukee. Green accepted, and the race was on!

The MOONLIGHT and PORTER hoisted sails and left Buffalo to begin the 800 mile journey. News of the race spread, and people became interested. Telegraphs flashed word ahead as to who was leading, and by how much. Wherever their route brought them close to shore, people came out to watch the two speedy vessels. Throughout the voyage the two schooners remained remarkably close. Finally, they passed through the straits of Mackinac and into Lake Michigan. The two vessels were now on the home stretch, but nature decided to intervene. A bad storm with high winds arose, and the going became dangerous. Captain Sullivan wisely, albeit somewhat uncharacteristically, elected to seek shelter near Port Washington. Captain Green, deciding that this was his chance chose to forego safety and push on. When the storm subsided a bit, the MOONLIGHT continued on to Milwaukee and there found her competitor waiting. The PORTER, however, was little more than a bare hull: no masts, no spars, no sails, no rigging! In fact, she was very lucky to still be afloat after the terrible storm chewed her up. The harbor tugs had found the PORTER drifting helplessly after the gale, and brought her into port. Evidently the two captains considered the 800 mile race a tie, and adjourned to a bar to celebrate the event together.[4]

The MOONLIGHT was no stranger to storms and over the years had ridden out her share. Once in September of 1896 she was blown high and dry up on shore near Marquette Michigan. On this occasion, though still a full-blooded sailing vessel, the MOONLIGHT, along with the HENRY A. KENT, was being towed by the CHARLES J. KERSHAW. The KERSHAW had engine trouble while running for the shelter of Marquette harbor, and ended up stranding on Chocolay Reef. The two schooners were thrown to the beach and remained there through the winter. In the spring of 1897 the MOONLIGHT and KENT were salvaged and repaired at considerable expense.

It was this same type of terrible storm which ended the MOONLIGHT'S career for good in 1903. By this time the Joseph C. Gilchrist Company of Cleveland had bought the boat, and converted it into a towbarge. Gilchrist was losing boats all over the Great Lakes in 1903, and the MOONLIGHT was added to the list on September 13th.

On Friday September 12th the 270 foot wooden steamer

The MOONLIGHT after being converted to a towbarge.
Richard J. Wright Great Lakes Marine Collection

The VOLUNTEER was towing the MOONLIGHT on her last voyage.

C. Patrick Labadie collection

VOLUNTEER towed the MOONLIGHT into Ashland to receive cargos of iron ore. Both vessels loaded at the Northwestern dock, the VOLUNTEER getting 2900 tons of ore, and the MOONLIGHT receiving 1400 tons. The cargo was consigned to Lake Erie ports. On Saturday Captain E.E. Campbell, who now skippered the MOONLIGHT, received his clearance papers, as did the VOLUNTEER'S captain. As they were preparing to leave a storm warning was issued, advising all vessels to stay in port. The two skippers complied, and decided to depart when the weather became more cooperative.

Sunday morning came and the VOLUNTEER and MOONLIGHT set out. The weather still was not good: winds were howling with considerable strength and heavy seas were running. The steamer and tow were making adequate headway however, and the men decided to push on. It was when the two vessels were approximately twelve miles east of Michigan Island that the trouble started. With the big waves battering her sides and breaking over her deck, the MOONLIGHT'S seams began to open up. With a full load of iron ore, the 29 year old vessel could not stand up to that kind of pounding. The VOLUNTEER was signalled and tried to come back alongside the MOONLIGHT. This proved to be very difficult under the gale-ridden conditions however. The MOONLIGHT was taking water fast, and time was running short. A fatal list and lurch, just as the VOLUNTEER drew near, proved to be the last dying gasps of the famous boat. With no time to spare the steamer pulled up next to her, and "the crew was taken off with great difficulty."[5] The towline was cut and the once mighty MOONLIGHT sounded and foundered. The schooner's crew was unharmed, and a piece of Great Lake's history was now entombed.

The VOLUNTEER continued on to Sault Ste. Marie, reported the loss, then steamed on to Lake Erie. The MOONLIGHT was valued at $12,000, less than half of what she was worth in her glory days. But the glorious era of the MOONLIGHTS, AURORAS and PORTERS were over. The graceful schooner was a symbol of a bygone period, and now she was gone. Fittingly, the MOONLIGHT — once one of the greatest freshwater sailing vessels — met her end on the greatest of the lakes, Superior.

Footnotes

1. William Mack was also part owner of the LUCERNE when she foundered off of Long Island in 1886.
2. Being neither a true barkentine or schooner, these ships were called either.
3. "Laker," the term used to differentiate Great Lakes vessels from ocean-going ships, is still widely used today.
4. Much of the above information was taken from James P. Barry's **Ships of the Great Lakes** and Harlan Hatcher's **The Great Lakes**. Both books provide the interested Great Lakes reader with a wealth of historical information.
5. ASHLAND DAILY PRESS, September 16, 1903.

MARQUETTE
Insured!

The word around the lake was that shipping baron Joseph C. Gilchrist had lost another one! The man's "wreck record" for 1903 had to inspire sympathy in even his bitterest rivals. Was it business genius or pure luck that had led him to insure his boats that season, after never having done so before? Either way, on October 15th, 1903 Gilchrist sadly chalked up another one: the MARQUETTE was now sailing the bottom a few miles east of Michigan Island.

The wooden steamer MARQUETTE was an oreboat, built in 1881. Her measurements were listed as 1,343 gross tons (1,117 net), with a 235 foot length and a 35 foot beam. She carried a crew of fourteen including Captain Charles N. Caughell. The veteran MARQUETTE had been plying the lakes as a member of the Gilchrist line for many years. When she went down, she was a total loss, but luckily, she was insured!

The Gilchrist fleet had never carried formal insurance, but had been "self-insured." The operators of the vessels would simply set aside a certain percentage of profit to cover loss or damage. A very persistent marine insurance salesman finally got the better of J.C. Gilchrist in 1903 however, and for the first time his boats were fully covered against all contingencies. Considering the way Lake Superior battered the Gilchrist boats that year, the shipowner from Cleveland made an incredibly wise move.

In July of that ill-fated year the Gilchrist steamer V. SWAIN sank at a Two Harbors dock, costing $12,000 to raise and repair it. In September the MOONLIGHT went down just east of the Apostles. Along with her cargo, the venerable schooner was worth over $12,000. Just two days after that the A.A. PARKER went down off of Grand Marais worth a total of $75,000. Then the veteran MARQUETTE met her doom, a $60,000 loss including cargo. Eleven days after the MARQUETTE'S demise, the MANHATTAN caught fire after stranding at Grand Island near Munising. The 252 foot steamer was a total loss worth $50,000, as was the 76,000 bushels of wheat she was carrying worth $65,000. In all, Lake Superior had rent

The Gilchrist Steamer MARQUETTE

damages to the Gilchrist fleet that year in excess of a quarter million dollars![1] History does not record the obvious trauma that a certain marine insurance salesman must have experienced that year...

At 4:00 Wednesday afternoon October 14th the MARQUETTE cleared Ashland. She had been loaded with 1,319 tons of iron ore at the Central oredock, and 700 tons at the Northwestern dock. The cargo was consigned to Lake Erie ports, but, of course, never made it. At 4:00 a.m., exactly twelve hours after pulling away from the Ashland docks, she was on the way down to her 34 fathom deep coffin.

All went well for the MARQUETTE for the first eight hours of the voyage. Even though fully loaded, she was making relatively good time. There was little or no sea and the weather conditions were perfect. Plodding on into the star-filled night the MARQUETTE gradually left the Apostles at her stern. At a point approximately twenty five miles east of Michigan Island, however, the hold was discovered to be taking on water. The twenty two year old steamer had sprung a leak! The captain immediately ordered the pumps started, and did a "180," completely reversing his course. The MARQUETTE was leaking badly, but Captain Caughell felt there might be adequate time to reach the islands and beach her.

Slowly but surely they were making their way back to the Apostles, hoping to win their race against time. At 2:45 in the morning it was decided that only the men needed to work the boat should remain on board. Ten of the crew then took a lifeboat and began rowing toward the island, while the captain, second engineer, second mate and watchman stayed. One hour went by and the vessel was closing in on Michigan Island, now only five miles away. Unfortunately, by this time, there was six feet of water in the hold and the pumps just couldn't control the inrushing sea. If the MARQUETTE could just stay afloat for awhile longer...

A few minutes before 4:00 a.m. it was becoming increasingly evident that the MARQUETTE just wasn't going to hold out. Suddenly, all three crewmembers yelled for the captain, and piled into the remaining lifeboat which had already been launched and tied alongside — the MARQUETTE was sinking! Captain Caughell later told the story:

We remained on the vessel long after we should have gotten off, and as a consequence nearly lost our lives. I felt the vessel shiver and ran and jumped into the boat on top of the others. The stern shot into the air and the pressure forced the mast out and it jumped straight into the air about twenty feet falling into the sea. Meanwhile we were frantically trying to get away, and when not over 100 feet away, the end came. The vessel broke in two just in front of the boiler. The decks blew up with the sound of an explosion of powder and the MARQUETTE sank head first. We came very nearly being drawn into the maelstrom, and it was only by the most desperate exertions that we kept from being sucked in and had great difficulty in keeping the small boat from overturning. I will never again stay on a vessel as long as I did this one.[2]

After the intense, terrifying moments were over, the four men settled in for a long period of pulling oars. They were, for the most part, out of danger, as the seas were calm and the skies clear. The other lifeboat wasn't even in sight, being so far ahead. The men rowed on as daybreak turned into sunny morning. Hours passed until finally, they neared the islands. Exhausted, they still decided to press on. At 3:30 in the afternoon, almost twenty four hours after they had left, the captain and three crewmembers arrived at Ashland. The men had been rowing for close to twelve hours and hadn't eaten anything for at least sixteen. They reported the loss of the MARQUETTE, and asked about their shipmates who, strangely enough, still hadn't shown up.

Two hours later, nine of the ten men arrived at Ashland aboard a tug, and they had a story to tell! After leaving the MARQUETTE the ten crewmembers rowed to the islands, opting to stop off at Madeline for a rest. They landed at 9:00 in the morning, obviously very tired after their six hour journey. After sizing up the situation they decided the best course of action would be to simply start out for Ashland. As they boarded the lifeboat one crewmember noticed that the fireman, Jens Johnson, was missing. At first it was thought that Johnson had merely wandered a short distance into the woods, so they called for him. No reply came however, and the nine men then started searching the surrounding woods. They looked for over two hours, but Jens Johnson was nowhere to be found! There was nothing they could do but shove off and head for Ashland, planning to return and continue the search later. A passing boat picked them up when just off the island, and brought them into port.

The missing fireman had been visibly shaken throughout the entire ordeal, and many crewmembers felt that the experience may have been too much for him to handle mentally. The newspaper reported the following:

Jens Johnson was left on Madeline Island, and it was feared that he had destroyed himself, as he showed great signs of fear when the boat began to fill and sink...During the trip (to Madeline) Johnson acted very nervous, and according to a story told by one of the crew this morning,

A drawing of the MARQUETTE breaking up.

Larry W. Hoopman

they had some difficulty in landing him safely on Madeline Island... Johnson was known to have a revolver on his person and great fear was felt, as his mind might have been jarred by his first wreck experience.[3]

Upon hearing this news from his crew, Captain Caughell decided to first grant the men their much needed rest, and organize a search party the next day. Caughell had lined up a boat to take the crew to Duluth the following afternoon, but there would be ample time to look for Johnson before that.

The following morning the captain selected George Foster, the watchman of the MARQUETTE, to go to Madeline and conduct a thorough search for the missing sailor. "He was to be joined at LaPointe by a party who will assist in searching the island in the hope of finding him alive," the newspaper observed.[4] The searchers began scouring the area, and before long found a live and healthy Johnson right where he was abandoned the previous day. Still a bit shaken mentally, he was "apparently not much the worse for his twenty hours experience on the island."[5] Johnson was brought to Ashland, and left for Duluth with the rest of the crew.

The MARQUETTE was a total loss of course, and still sails the bottom some five miles east of Michigan Island. She lay, along with several other ships, as somewhat of a testimonial to the foresight — or luck — belonging to Joseph C. Gilchrist. She is also fitting testimony to the year 1903, when Lake Superior simply swallowed part of the Gilchrist fleet.

Footnotes
1. Two other Gilchrist vessels, the JOHN CRAIG and the WAVERLY were also lost that year on other lakes.
2. ASHLAND DAILY PRESS, October 16, 1903.
3. Ibid.
4. Ibid.
5. Ibid.

THE NOQUE BAY
A Stockton Blaze

It was 7:00 the evening of October 9, 1905 that Jack Hedlund, a local fisherman, returned to his dock in Bayfield. Jack had been out checking his nets, but the stories he brought back to town that day did not concern fishing. He had spotted a large boat burning near the shore in Julian Bay of Stockton Island. Venturing closer Hedlund recognized the deceased vessel to be the NOQUE BAY, a tow barge that had recently been in Bayfield. He saw no signs of life anywhere, nor did he see the NOQUE BAY'S usual consorts the LIZZIE MADDEN and the MAUTENEE.

The steamer MADDEN towing her barges NOQUE BAY and MAUTENEE were a familiar sight to the Chequamegon Bay area. The three boats, owned by T.H. Madden of Bay City, Michigan, stopped there regularly to pick up lumber and other goods. In Apostle Island waters in November of 1900 the LIZZIE MADDEN actually "came very near going to the bottom of Lake Superior in a gale," the Ashland paper had reported.[1] Pulling her usual tows she had caught on fire, but luckily was saved. Five years later, ironically, it was the NOQUE BAY which ended her sailing days there, due to fire.

On October 3rd the Comstock and Wilcox Company of Ashland loaded the NOQUE BAY in Bayfield with 600,000 feet of hemlock lumber. There she waited six days for the MADDEN and MAUTENEE to come from Duluth. On the morning of October 9th the three boats pulled away from Bayfield heading for Buffalo to deliver their cargo. Twenty miles out of port the NOQUE BAY was discovered to be on fire. It was exactly twelve noon and the whole crew was eating lunch when smoke was first smelled. The fire had started in the forward part of the ship in the donkey boiler room, and had gained much headway by the time it was discovered.[2] It became readily apparent that the blaze could not be successfully fought, so the MADDEN quickly headed toward Stockton and beached her tow. The crew managed to dump some of the cargo overboard, then jump the burning vessel and climb safely aboard the MADDEN. Several hundred thousand feet of hemlock must have

The NOQUE BAY loaded with lumber.   Ken Thro Collection

been an incredible fire!

There was nothing the MADDEN could do so they continued downbound with only the MAUTENEE in tow. When they reached the Portage Canal at Sault Ste. Marie they wired ahead to Buffalo, then contacted Ashland with the news. This was the first official word that the Chequamegon area received, but most people by that time already knew of Jack Hedlund's story.

In 1900 when the LIZZIE MADDEN was a few miles east of Stockton Island, a lamp exploded below decks and a huge fire ensued. It was exactly midnite and the crews happened to be changing. It proved extremely lucky that the entire crew of four-teen were awake and on deck because it took every last man to help extinquish the blaze. In the words of the captain: "There was such a gale blowing that the NOQUE BAY and MAUTENEE could not come up alongside us. Had our fight against the fire been hopeless, we all would have perished."[3] Two men actually passed out from the smoke and almost died, but were for-tunately revived. The MADDEN suffered damages of over $2000. Five years later her tow was a total loss.

The well-known Captain Cornelius Flynn of Duluth sailed out to the NOQUE BAY a few days after the accident was reported. No stranger to Apostle Island waters, he had seen his own boat, the R.G. STEWART, wrecked on Michigan Island some years earlier. Flynn managed to successfully salvage the anchors from the NOQUE BAY, and approximately 175,000 feet of lumber that the crew had jettisoned. The ship itself, worth $7000 to her owners, was nothing more than a blackened hull.

The NOQUE BAY was built in Trenton, Michigan in 1872. She was 205 feet long and listed 684 tons as her gross weight. She was originally built as a schooner, but like so many sailboats of that period finished her days as a towbarge after being converted by the Madden Company. The burnt remains of the NOQUE BAY still lay in Julian Bay in shallow water.

The steamer LIZZIE MADDEN — in 1900 she almost ended her career in the Apostles.
C. Patrick Labadie Collection

Footnotes
1. ASHLAND DAILY PRESS, November 19, 1900.
2. A donkey engine is a small auxiliary steam engine used for hoisting or pumping on board a ship.
3. ASHLAND DAILY PRESS, November 19, 1900.

SEVONA
Courage and Death

She was a proud vessel, relatively large for her day. Her captain was as experienced a shipmaster as could be found on the Great Lakes. She even had the distinction of owning the first electric searchlight ever used on America's inland oceans. But she sailed out into an angry Superior one day, and within a mere twenty four hours became a part of history. The swirling seas and the unholy Apostles decided to have their way with her. It was in September of 1905 that the SEVONA met her fate.

The SEVONA was built in 1890 at West Bay City, Michigan. She was launched as the EMILY P. WEED that year with an overall length of 300 feet. In 1898 she changed owners and was rechristened the SEVONA. The big steamer was of steel construction, and was used mainly as an oreboat. In late fall of 1904 the SEVONA sailed into a Buffalo shipyard to receive a facelift. That winter the big freighter became even bigger, being cut in half and fitted with a seventy three foot long section added to her midships. The sturdy steamer now had a gross weight of 3166 tons (a net of 2258), a length of 373 feet, a beam of 41 feet, and a 21 foot depth. She received new boilers, an electric light plant, and that distinctive electric searchlight set on the bridge. These renovations were obviously quite costly, but James McBrier the head of the SEVONA'S company had confidence in her. The SEVONA was now the pride of the McBrier fleet. As she steamed out of the Buffalo harbor in June of 1905, she was practically a brand new ship...but the newness wouldn't last for long.

It was 6:03 the evening of September 1st, 1905 when the SEVONA pulled away from the Allouez docks in West Superior, Wisconsin. She was downbound for her home port of Erie Pennsylvania loaded with 6000 tons of iron ore. Heavy ground swells were running as she left the harbor, but there was no wind and the weather bureau forecast was good. At the wheel was Captain Donald Sutherland McDonald, a Scots-Canadian originally from the Lake Ontario shore. McDonald had been a seaman since his youth, and had been one of only two sur-

95

The once mighty SEVONA.

vivors in a terrible shipwreck on the Irish coast many years earlier. In time he returned to fresh water and was now a respected skipper and part owner of the SEVONA. Aboard the ship were a crew of twenty four including four women. Mrs. William Phillipie, wife of the chief engineer was along, as was Mrs. C.H. (Louise) Clucky, the cook's wife. Two young ladies, Miss Kate Spencer and Miss Lillian Jones were on board as guests of the McBrier Family. As the SEVONA left Superior the two guests were thrilled, eagerly looking forward to this Great Lakes crossing. Little did they know that they were sailing into a Superior storm which would claim four ships — including their own.

All went well for the ill-fated vessel during the first few hours after departure. A nice supper and pleasant conversation were enjoyed by the skipper and his guests in the elegantly decorated dining room. At 9:00 p.m. the two young ladies retired to their cabins in the forward end of the ship, and Captain McDonald went back to ship's business. It was at about this time that the wind started to rise dramatically. The blow was sweeping in across the open sea and continued to gather strength with each passing hour. By midnite she was howling at full gale force: this was definitely a dreaded Superior northeaster. By 2:00 a.m. the SEVONA was some seventy miles out of port, boring into very heavy seas that broke over the bow and ran the full length of her deck. The situation was so bad that Captain McDonald — figuring that he was an hour or so past Sand Island — decided to turn and head southwest toward the Apostles in hopes of finding shelter. The crew was notified of the decision, and the captain woke the young ladies

The stern section a few days after the wreck.

Ken Thro Collection

telling them to "put breakable stuff in a secure place as when the boat put about she would toss badly" in the words of Kate Spencer.[1]

The SEVONA ran before the wild storm. At 3:30 a.m. Captain McDonald again woke the sleeping ladies and told them to get dressed: the situation had worsened. At 4:15 a.m. he had the ladies don lifejackets and ordered four seamen to take them aft to the galley. Hanging on to lifelines the sailors escorted the women to the rear of the ship through waist deep waves that washed over the deck. The forward end of the ship had apparently started taking on some water, and the two lifeboats that the SEVONA carried were both aft. The captain evidently wanted his guests to be as close to the lifeboats as possible.

The big freighter plowed on through high seas in hopes of finding shelter, but the pounding rain made visibility almost nonexistent. About 5:45 a.m. Captain McDonald realized that they must be near the Apostles and slowed his engines to half speed. Having made a calculated guess as to the SEVONA'S location, the captain ordered the men in the wheelhouse to keep a sharp lookout for either Sand or Raspberry Island lights. The storm was so severe however, that nobody on the bridge saw any island or light, and the SEVONA steamed on. Fifteen minutes later, still running blind, the SEVONA struck. With three distinct, sickening crashes the big boat came to a halt on Sand Island Shoal. The damage was extensive: a gaping hole in the bow, and a split in the center of the hull. The SEVONA was now in two pieces.

Engulfed in the awesome storm and battered by huge waves the SEVONA now lay helpless. Captain McDonald, completely cut off from the stern section by the break in the hull, barked orders through a megaphone to the men aft. Shouting into the wind, he directed them to lower a lifeboat and put the women into it, but to hang on to the freighter as long as possible. Chief Engineer William Phillipi was now in charge of the aft end of the ship, and coordinated the effort of carrying out the captain's orders. Having succeeded in getting the starboard boat into the water, Phillipi directed the men to hold it there in the lee of the wreck as best they could. Kate Spencer later recalled the terrifying events:

> I cannot think or talk of the wreck without shudder following shudder. At about 6:00 came the terrible crash which broke the vessel in two. We got into the lifeboats at that time, but the captain and the other men could not come aft owing to the break. He hailed us through the megaphone 'Hang on as long as you can.' We did so but the sea was pounding so hard that Chief Engineer Phillipi finally directed us out of the small boat and into the large vessel again, all congregating in the dining room which

The deck of the SEVONA after the wreck.

View of the wrecked SEVONA stern section.

Ken Thro Collection

*was still intact. The big boat was pounding and tossing.
Now a piece of the deck would go and then a portion of
the dining room. During all this time the men forward
could not get to us.²*

Well aware of the fact that both lifeboats were aft, the "men
forward" (seven of them including the captain) set about
building a raft from wooden hatch covers and doors. Long
minutes passed into hours. The ship's whistle was blown for
help until the fires under the boilers were extinguished — then
the rocket flares were sent up until they were all gone. The
distress signals of the storm battered SEVONA were all in vain
however. There was no help available.

It was at 11:00 a.m. — with the awesome storm still howling
as furiously as ever — that the final breakup of the aft section
seemed imminent. The skylight in the dining room had been
shattered and the water was now knee high. Supplies from the
galley and pantry began to wash through and piece by piece

Advertisement for SEVONA excursion.

the beautiful oak paneling began to burst in from the pounding seas. The time had come to leave the SEVONA. Kate Spencer later remembered:

> *Everything seemed to be breaking at once, and by order of the Chief Engineer we took to the small boat again. One by one we piled into the boat leaving six men behind us. I never heard such a heart rending cry as came from those six. 'For God's sake, don't leave us!' they cried. So two of our men got out and helped the six pull the port boat over to the starboard side and launch it. Then we both set out. It was a terrible fight to keep the small boat afloat!*[3]

Phillipi took charge of the larger boat, while deckhand Charles Scouller, who had some small boat experience, took charge of the other. In Phillipi's boat were the four women, Cluckey the cook, assistant engineer Adam Fiden and his son, and three firemen, Otto Schmidt, Neil Nelson and Gretten Rettner. Joining Scouller were William Long, Paul Stockel, Edgar Ryder, George Slade and the one armed oiler Harry Van Vlack. Unfortunately all the experienced seamen were isolated in the forward end, meaning the lifeboats were crewed by people who knew little or nothing about handling small vessels. Phillipi attempted to maneuver his boat towards the forward section, but the huge waves rolling over the SEVONA's broken center kept washing the little craft away and threatening to swamp it. Finally, with the rain pouring down and the high seas tossing the tiny boat at will, Phillipi gave up and cast off, his makeshift crew frantically pulling at the oars.

The lifeboats seemed no more than insignificant toys in the swirling Superior seas. Rowing proved completely ineffective in these awesome walls of water, and the boat's occupants could do nothing more than bail water to help their cause. Under these nightmarish circumstances Phillipi's crew survived for six terror filled hours. The Ashland Daily Press later reported the crew to be "alternately despairing and hopeful. At times they would pray for their lives, while they were bailing the small craft of the spray which came aboard constantly."[4] At first they thought they might be able to reach York Island, but were blown helplessly by it. Hours later (five miles from where they left the SEVONA) the lifeboat came close to the mainland, but was unmercifully greeted with sharp rocks and steep cliffs. The crew beat along the shore, trying desperately to stay clear of the rocky dangers until, luckily, they spotted a sand beach. They attempted to maneuver close, but the huge waves still had the final say. Miraculously, at just the right moment, a big roller picked up the tiny boat and hurled it up on the beach. The exhausted but thankful crew crawled away from the mad waters.

The second lifeboat was "doing very badly as she left the SEVONA" in the words of Phillipi. They were likewise totally at the mercy of Superior's savagery. Scouller took the tiller the whole time, and one-armed Van Vlack never once stopped bailing with his cap. The six men in the smaller boat "had a terrible trip," in the words of one of the deckhands. "None of us were sailors and all we could do was to keep the boat headed into the wind to keep from swamping. We finally landed or were blown ashore on Sand Island..."[5] As soon as the six were thrown from the boat, the next breaking wave demolished the small craft. Luck it seems, or God, was with both crews.

A homesteader, who was out in the gale looking for a missing cow, spotted the crew of Phillipi's boat shortly after they were thrown ashore. He directed them to the nearest shelter which was approximately two miles away. Exhausted, cold and hungry the eleven completed the arduous trek as quickly as they could, pressed by the knowledge that the captain and six men were still aboard the ship. When they reached the cabin of lumberman Napolean "Nap" Rabideaux they were offered dry clothes and hot food. Aching muscles and minor cuts and bruises were luckily the only injuries suffered by the brave crew.

After a brief rest Phillipi knew he must press on to Bayfield in hopes of finding help for his captain and mates. Guided by Rabideaux, Phillipi set out with a team of horses and a wagon.

As the newspaper reported later: "Only the person that has travelled that almost untrodden country can appreciate the difficulties of the trip."[6] It took the better part of a day to reach Bayfield, the two men literally having to clear a road because of the almost 200 windfalls that occurred during the storm. Upon reaching Bayfield Phillipi enlisted the help of fifteen men and the tug HARROW to go out to the wreck. It took over two hours in the teeth of the gusting northeaster to reach the site. As they approached the SEVONA Phillipi's heart sank. He looked out over the waters and saw only the battered remains of the SEVONA'S aft section. Approximately 100 feet of broken steel was all that was left of the once proud ship. The forward two-thirds of the vessel was completely gone... claimed victim by the Superior seas. There was absolutely no sign of Captain McDonald and the other six seamen. Dejectedly, the HARROW turned back for Bayfield...

The following day news of the six men in the other lifeboat reached Bayfield. After being blown ashore on Sand Island the men found an abandoned cabin for shelter. Shortly thereafter they were discovered by a fisherman who provided them with food. With the storm subsiding Phillipi was able to secure the services of a larger tug, the R.W. CURRIE, and pick up the stranded Sand Island survivors. There were no serious injuries suffered by the six.

Happily reunited with their chief engineer, the crew of Scouller's boat immediately asked as to the fate of their captain. Phillipi could only tell them what he had seen when he had reached the SEVONA. The mystery of the seven deck-bound comrades remained. Did the captain — as in the old shipwreck tales — bravely go down with his ship? Did the seven men attempt an escape from the ill-fated SEVONA? Was there cause for that faint glimmer of hope that they washed ashore on another island?

These questions were soon to be answered by Mr. Emanuel Lueck, the Sand Island lighthouse keeper, who watched the entire disaster with binoculars. He, in fact, saw the big freighter go onto the reef (some of the SEVONA crew reported seeing the dim light of Sand Island immediately after the crash), and heard the distress signals, but could do nothing to help. Lueck watched the two lifeboats set out, but lost sight of them in the thundering waves. Later, with visibility improving, he saw the bow section of the SEVONA beginning to list. McDonald and the men came out of the wheelhouse and prepared to launch the makeshift wooden raft they had built. With this dramatic scene unfolding in front of his eyes, Lueck was entirely helpless to offer assistance: he could do nothing but watch. The bow section suddenly gave out just as the men

The Sand Island lighthouse keeper, Emanuel Lueck, who helplessly watched the entire tragedy unfold.

climbed onto the raft and shoved off. The brave seven desperately clung to their "lifeboat" as the huge waves pounded over them time and again. They fought gallantly against tremendous odds — each man hanging onto the others so none would be washed overboard. Miraculously, the tiny raft closed in on Sand Island. Lueck prayed...It looked like they were going to make it! As the men neared the beach, enormous breakers suddenly tore the raft to shreds. Lueck fervently scanned the water but saw...no one. All seven men — who had fought so long and so hard — were sucked under and beaten to death by the cruel seas.

In time the bodies of all those who had been on the bow section were found along Sand Island beach. The Ashland newspaper reported the discovery of four bodies (including Captain McDonald) on September 6th, 1905: "The bodies recovered were horribly pounded up on the logs and driftwood on the beach but their faces are all sufficiently clear to allow for easy identification."[7]

With the recovery of Captain McDonald's body, another mystery of sorts sprang up. The Captain was known to be carrying $1500 on his person for the purpose of conducting ship's business. When checked however, there was absolutely no money on him — yet all the other articles he was known to be carrying were still in place. If Superior hadn't claimed any

The SEVONA Memorial Cottage, built from the salvaged timbers of the wrecked vessel.   Bayfield Heritage Association

other possessions of the captain's, how would she rip exactly $1500 from him? The seachers looked for hours, but could only come up with a single dollar bill found on the beach next to McDonald's body. The answer to this mystery supposedly was to be found in Bayfield in the weeks following the shipwreck. It seems that a few shady characters ("undesirables," as they were called) were seen frequenting the bars and shops spending huge sums of money, some of it partially mutilated and watersoaked. When asked, they never could account for their "windfall" satisfactorily. The local explanation was simple: they had found McDonald's body before the recovery crew did.

Three men were actually arrested and brought to trial before Judge A.M. Warden in Bayfield. On November 8, the trial date, Sheriff H.J. Conlin produced the prisoners, but the prosecuting attorney never showed up! Defense attorney E.C. Alvord pled his case, and the men were set free due to lack of evidence.

With four ships and many lives lost in this awesome September storm, public outcry was swift. Seamen and concerned citizens alike demanded better lighthouses, more shoals buoys, a local lifesaving station, telephones (or at least telegraphs) to some of the islands, and rescue boats with more men stationed at the lighthouses. Many sailors and maritime engineers questioned the process of lengthening the big oreboats, claiming that the SEVONA'S hull split right where the new section had been added. Some demands were met, others were not. In November of 1905 the SEVONA'S certificate of enrollment was surrendered. She was valued at $220,000, but insured for only $160,000. The pride of the McBrier fleet was a total loss.

Interestingly enough a former Lieutenant Governor of Wisconsin, Samuel Fifield of Ashland, had a summer resort on Sand Island, and salvaged some of the SEVONA wreckage. With this, he actually built a house and named it the "Sevona Memorial Cottage" in honor of the dead ship. For years guests who visited the famous resort were housed in the sturdy little dwelling. Today the Sevona Cottage still stands on Sand Island, having recently undergone renovation.

On a calm day in July of 1909 the government steamer VIDETTE sailed out to the wreck of the SEVONA. What was left of the old ship was blown up with a quarter ton of dynamite, as the vessel itself had become a dangerous navigational hazard. The SEVONA was now a memory — sailing only in the minds of the men that once worked her, and the people that remembered the big ship with that distinctive electric search light...[8]

Footnotes

1. DULUTH HERALD, September 5, 1905.
2. ASHLAND DAILY PRESS, September 5, 1905.
3. Ibid.
4. ASHLAND DAILY PRESS, September 5, 1905.
5. Ibid.
6. DULUTH HERALD, September 11, 1905.
7. ASHLAND DAILY PRESS, September 6, 1905.
8. For additional information on Captain McDonald and/or the SEVONA tragedy, see Dwight Boyer's excellent chapter "A Scot Comes Home for the Harvest" in the book **True Tales of the Great Lakes.**

PRETORIA
One of the Largest

It was a well known fact that veteran boat owner and builder Captain James Davidson never carried insurance. The shipping magnate from Michigan had endured over forty years of Great Lakes activities without a single accident! Considering the large number of boats he had owned over the years and the volatile nature of these waters, this was truly a remarkable record. By his own estimate he had saved over $1,000,000 in premium all tolled. This perfect record came to a fatal end however, in that storm bedeviled year of 1905. The same September tempest which sank the SEVONA also laid claim to a Davidson ship. The magnificent schooner PRETORIA was cruelly brought to her knees just off of Outer Island.

The PRETORIA was one of the largest sailing vessels ever to have operated on the Great Lakes. The 2,790 ton wooden three-master was built in 1900 at West Bay City, Michigan. She was an impressive 338 feet in length with a 44 foot beam and 23 foot depth. Captain Davidson always liked to do things in a big way, and this schooner was no exception.

On Friday, September 1st the PRETORIA was loaded with iron ore at the Allouez docks in Superior. Another Davidson boat, the wooden steamer VENEZUELA, was to rendezvous with the schooner that morning, pick her up and tow her downbound to Lake Erie. The 263 foot VENEZUELA had cleared Ashland the previous Wednesday, then had steamed up to Two Harbors to receive her cargo. The steamer and consort left Superior as scheduled late Friday morning. Of definite irony is the fact that the SEVONA received her load shortly after the PRETORIA, at the very same docks. Both vessels would be dealt fatal blows the very next day in the Apostle Islands, when a legendary gale would send them to the bottom.

The ominous storm approached as the VENEZUELA and PRETORIA sailed on through the day and into the night. The weather worsened as the ships neared the Apostles, but they decided to push on and bypass shelter. As they skirted the northern flank of the islands the furious northeaster hurled violent waves at the boats' timbers. Still, the staunch and stub-

The PRETORIA being launched sideways — a Great Lakes tradition. Ralph K. Roberts Collection

born steamer VENEZUELA plodded on into open water — making, as it turned out, a fatal mistake. At 7:30 in the morning, thirty miles past the last point of refuge, Outer Island, the PRETORIA'S steering gear failed. Captain Charles Smart signalled the VENEZUELA, and the steamer immediately turned towards the Apostles. At 8:00 the towline between the two vessels could stand the stress and strain no longer; it snapped at both ends, falling irretrievably into the water.

By this time visibility was greatly diminished, and the big schooner started to drift. The VENEZUELA searched desperately for her tow, but couldn't find her. In the gale force winds and slashing seas a rescue may have been impossible at this point anyway. Regretfully, the VENEZUELA gave up her search and decided to save herself. She had a very rough time of it, but eventually found her way into sheltered Chequamegon Bay. For the PRETORIA, this was the beginning of the end.

On board the storm-tossed schooner Captain Charles Smart now found himself in the middle of a mariner's nightmare. Heavily laden with ore, the boat rode low in the water, making her an easy target for the enormous waves which crashed over her deck. Blinding rain was driven by the winds of a freshwater hurricane. Sizing up the grim situation Smart realized that there were only a few courses of action available to him. He quickly ordered a sail raised at the bow in hopes of gaining some maneuverability. It held for only a few minutes before the wicked winds tore it to shreds. The anchor was then dropped in an attempt to halt the ship's drift, but it simply dragged. The pumps were started in an effort to control the water which had begun to penetrate the hatch combings. For a short while they held their own, but it was just a matter of time before the seas battered in some of the hatch covers. The water level in the hold slowly but steadily rose with each inrushing wave. There was hopelessly little left that Captain Smart could do. The powerless PRETORIA was totally at the mercy of an enraged Superior.

There was precious little visibility, yet the captain and crew could easily see that they had a date with destiny in the Apostles. Time was now being measured in hours, and the relentless northeaster was constantly pushing the PRETORIA towards the islands. Perhaps the ship would be blown into the lee of one of the Apostles, meaning safety and salvation for both boat and crew; or — with equal odds unfortunately — she might be thrown aground on a shoal and there battered to bits by breaking waves. By midafternoon, the verdict was still out.

With a slight improvement in visibility Captain Smart was finally able to distinguish a dark band looming out of the gray. By 4:00 in the afternoon the PRETORIA had come to within two miles of Outer Island — her crew still laboring at the pumps and keeping the boat afloat. The present course though, meant certain grounding. This close proximity to the island meant that the ship was in shallower water however, and Captain Smart reasoned that the anchor might hold better here. Perhaps the PRETORIA could ride out this god-awful gale yet.

The PRETORIA at dock.

C. Patrick Labadie Collection

The steamer VENEZUELA lost its tow PRETORIA in the gale.
Richard J. Wright Collection

"When the ship had arrived within one and a half miles of Outer Island I saw that it was in bad shape, but thought it might possibly stand it if I threw out the anchor" Smart later recalled. "I knew it would go to pieces if it went ashore."[1]

The anchor was dropped and this time it held. Unfortunately the distressed schooner was now in for some severe punishment. The heavy seas pounded the PRETORIA'S hull without reprieve. More hatch coverings caved in, then the entire covering board was washed away. The riotous seas rushed into the ship. The pumps, of little use now, finally quit. Suddenly a battered deck house was beaten off by a big roller, and the decks themselves began to float away. Piece by broken piece Superior was laying claim to her prey. The captain and his nine man crew knew that there was only one option left: abandon ship!

At 4:35 p.m. the mighty PRETORIA began to sink. Ten minutes later her hull was resting on an even keel in 52 feet of water, with only the three masts visible above the surface. Just before the final plunge the ten men boarded the lifeboat, shoved off and started for shore. The thundering waves tossed the tiny boat about, but good progress toward land was being made. One mile and many anxious minutes later the small craft was still afloat. The men watched with hopeful eyes as they closed in on Outer Island — but Superior had not surrendered yet. Four hundred feet from shore the lifeboat was riding the crest of a wave, but then the raging surf took control. Captain Smart remembered, "At last a gigantic wave struck us

110

and we were thrown overboard, some of the crew being thrown ten feet into the air. At one time or another every one of the ten men were clinging to the overturned boat, but they dropped off one by one..."[2]

Four exhausted men eventually slipped under the boiling seas to surface no more. The other six, still fighting for their lives, desperately hung on to their only hope for salvation. Gasping for air and struggling for life they continued toward shore until "we were so close to land that it seemed as if two or three more big seas would carry us right on to shore. Then a sailor named Lindloff started to swim the remaining few feet, but sunk before our eyes..."[3]

Five men were now dead within a few hundred feet of land, and it was far from certain that the remaining five could save themselves. With what little strength they had left the men struggled on until, suddenly, salvation surprisingly appeared. Seemingly from out of nowhere a sixty year old man rushed into the mad waters — with complete disregard for his own life — and one by one pulled all five survivors to safety. Not unlike Emanuel Lueck and the Sand Island SEVONA incident the light keeper John Irvine had watched the whole tragic accident unfold from the tower. The Duluth newspaper reported: "Captain Irvine, who, though sixty years old, is still hale and strong, started to their rescue. By almost superhuman effort, while his life was endangered every minute, he brought the five who still clung to the lifeboat safely to shore."[4]

The grateful men were housed and fed by Irvine and his wife for two days. On Monday, September 4th the steamer VENEZUELA, out looking for her lost tow, was signalled to the island and picked up the survivors. They were brought to Bayfield, then Ashland, and on to their respective homes. A few days later the newspapers carried this information:

> The names of the survivors are as follows:
> Charles Smart, master, West Bay City
> Charles Fierman, mate, West Bay City
> William Smart, seaman, West Bay City
> Oscar Orling, seaman, Milwaukee
> Ned Blank, seaman, Buffalo
> The dead:
> Henry Schwartz, donkey engineman, West Bay City
> Axel Lindloff, seaman, Marinette
> Isaac Myers, seaman, Milwaukee
> Alfred Pebsal, Seaman, Sweden
> Steward, colored, unknown, shipped at Duluth.[5]

In time, all the bodies of those that died washed up on Outer Island, and were recovered.

The PRETORIA was only five years old when she went down.

She carried an A1 rating, the highest attainable, but was obviously no match for the relentless seas which pursued her that September day. In time, the big lake beat her down even more, knocking the masts into the water and strewing wreckage all over the bottom. Some years ago the ship's bell was discovered in shallow water near Outer Island, verifying the crewmember's reports that the deck had been stripped from the boat when she foundered.

After forty three years of accident-free shipping Captain James Davidson suffered a major setback that dire day. The uninsured PRETORIA was a total loss estimated at $60,000. The final legacy of that legendary storm in the Apostle Islands was twelve brave men dead, and two proud ships down.

Footnotes

1. ASHLAND DAILY PRESS, Sept. 5, 1905.
2. Ibid.
3. ASHLAND DAILY PRESS, Sept. 18, 1905.
4. DULUTH NEWS TRIBUNE, Sept. 5, 1905.
5. DULUTH HERALD, Sept. 5, 1905.

IRA H. OWEN
Went Missing

There will always be fierce arguments as to which November storm was the worst: Huron's of 1913, Michigan's of 1940, or Superior's of 1905. In loss of life and in complete loss of long steel ships, the Huron storm has no equal; in windgust velocity and in wave sharpness, the Michigan storm may take the palm; but in combined terms of snow, cold, wind, shipwreck and heavy seas, the Superior storm is generally agreed to be the worst ever to strike the Great Lakes. In what seemed minutes the temperature dropped to 12 degrees below zero, and a hurricane ripped the world of freshwater apart. During the last three days of November the wind went around the clock at 70 to 80 miles an hour. Mountainous seas rolled and thundered between Duluth and the Soo Canal.
William Ratigan in **Great Lakes Shipwrecks & Survivals**

The legendary storm of November 1905 wreaked havoc and destruction all up and down the greatest of the Great Lakes. When the final tally was in, the count was 78 seamen dead and 30 vessels wrecked. The Apostles unfortunately saw their share of action during the "big blow." The huge flagship of the Pittsburgh Steamship Line, the WILLIAM E. COREY, impaled itself on Gull Island Reef running for shelter. Twelve full days later she was pulled free with damages amounting to $100,000. A costly stranding, but luckily no one was killed. The greatest loss of life anywhere during the Superior storm however occurred close by, just east of Outer Island. A full crew of nineteen men perished with their ship when the IRA H. OWEN "went missing."

The IRA OWEN was considered an especially staunch and seaworthy vessel. She was owned by the National Steamship Company of Chicago, and was a familiar sight on Superior. Built in 1887 in Cleveland she was one of the earliest steel steamers on the Great Lakes, uniquely sporting twin stacks. The OWEN was 262 feet long, 1,753 tons burden, and carried a small 750 horsepower engine. She was captained by Joseph

The twin-stacker IRA H. OWEN.

Mulligan, a veteran lake skipper "...well known at every important port."[1] On board for the season's final voyage of 1905 was another famous captain also, Thomas Honner. The ill-fated trip proved to be the OWEN'S final voyage...period.

On the morning of November 28, 1905 the IRA OWEN Left Duluth downbound with a load of barley. The weather was worsening as she passed the Apostles, but Captain Mulligan decided against seeking shelter at this point. As she was steaming by Outer Island the furious gale picked up and started pounding the OWEN mercilessly. Enormous seas swelled, temperatures dropped below zero, hurricane force winds whipped the driving snow — and the IRA OWEN found herself in open water with no place of refuge in sight. Deperately the brave crew fought the wild seas as best they could. At the height of the terrible storm Captain Alva Keller of the steamer HAROLD B. NYE spotted the OWEN. She appeared to be in dire straits and was constantly blowing distress signals, but the 380 foot NYE was in so much trouble herself that she couldn't possibly lend assistance. The dense snow squall then descended upon the OWEN, completely blotting her from Keller's view. The NYE continued to ride out the monstrous waves for two hours when, slowly, the squall lifted and faint visibility was restored. Keller immediately grabbed his binoculars and pointed them in the direction where he last sighted the OWEN. Anxiously, tensely, he scanned the water, but saw nothing. The IRA H. OWEN had vanished.

A full two days later the HAROLD B. NYE miraculously limped into the port of Two Harbors, Minnesota with considerable damage suffered. Keller had a terrible feeling about the OWEN, but he could not be sure of anything. On December 1st the fate of the OWEN was finally revealed. Captain M.K. Chamberlain of the steamer SIR WILLIAM SIEMENS sailed into Ashland with bad news. At 10:00 that morning twelve miles east of Michigan Island he sailed through some wreckage that included chairs, the top of a cabin, and a number of life preservers marked "S.S. IRA H. OWEN." Upon receiving this news the ship's owners pronounced the loss of the IRA OWEN a certainty.

Captain J.J. Keith the manager of the National Steamship Company later spoke of the incident:

"I do not understand what could have happened to the OWEN. She had a cargo of 116,000 bushels of barley, which was a light load for the ship. I spent three days in Duluth before the OWEN sailed, seeing that everything was in the best of condition. The hatch fastenings were all overhauled and made as strong as they could be. Why the steamer should have met disaster will always remain

a mystery I fear, for there is no hope that any of the crew are still alive."[2]

Interesting to note is the fact that the wreckage sighted by the SIEMENS contained a number of life preservers. Did any of the crew don life jackets, or did the ship go down so fast that the sailors had no time to reach them? Since no bodies were ever found the question will probably remain unanswered. The exact location, time or reason for the OWEN'S sinking was never discovered. Perhaps the mountainous walls of water simply swallowed her, or possibly the cargo suddenly shifted with the rolling seas and she listed badly, or maybe she was pounded to pieces and just broke up...

The OWEN was fully insured for $100,000, and her cargo was also insured. This is no consolation of course when a proud vessel goes down with all hands. November 28, 1905 was indeed a grim day in Superior's shipping history, with the darkest hour occurring just east of the Apostles when nineteen men died with the IRA H. OWEN.

Artist's conception of the IRA H. OWEN'S demise.

Larry W. Hoopman

Footnotes
1. ASHLAND DAILY PRESS, Dec. 2, 1905.
2. Ibid.

OTTAWA
The Famous Reid Wrecker

When she was launched in 1881, the BOSCOBEL was the largest tug on the Great Lakes. She was 151 feet in length, 28 feet in beam and 13 feet in depth. Her massive 600 horsepower engine was bigger than that carried by many freighters in those days. When she went down almost thirty years later, the mighty tug was still one of the largest and most powerful boats of her kind anywhere on the lakes.

The tug was later rechristened the OTTAWA, by which name she is best known. She was built in Chicago and had a gross tonnage of 610.8. Originally the boat was used for rafting logs on Lake Michigan, but in 1901 was bought (and renamed) by the well-known Reid Wrecking Company of Sarnia Ontario. The OTTAWA was captained by J.F. Reid, son of Captain James Reid, the company's owner. The tug participated in many rescues and salvage operations on Lake Superior under the Reid Company, and became quite a famous vessel. As a matter of fact, pulling an impaled steamer off a reef and bringing her to safety was the OTTAWA'S last mission.

On a storm-plaqued November 13th, 1909 the big steamer JAMES H. HOYT had a spell of miserable luck. While passing the Apostles the HOYT'S engines became disabled, and the 353 foot freighter found itself drifting towards Outer Island. Finally the HOYT was tossed onto an uncharted ledge about two miles northeast of the island, thereby stranding with no protection from the furious wind and sea. Captain Charles Ainsworth ordered First Mate William Chamberlain and several others to launch the lifeboat and seek assistance. After a terrible 13 hour ride the little boat reached Bayfield, and the men made a plea for help. Three tugs and a lighter went out to see what could be done. They worked all day in the nasty conditions, lightering the cargo of iron ore and pulling on the HOYT, but to no avail. The boats returned to port with the steamer's crew. They went out the following day, but their efforts were again in vain. The salvagers tried to free the HOYT for a full week with no luck. Finally, the big boat was turned over to the underwriters, who contacted the Reid Wrecking

The steamer OTTAWA

Company. The OTTAWA and MANISTIQUE were brought down from Ontario and put to work on the HOYT. It took the two wrecking boats along with another tug, over a week themselves to free the steamer. On November 29th the HOYT was released, and brought to shelter in Red Cliff Bay waters.[1] The salvage and repair bill for the battered boat was $65,000.

After a successful but exhausting day the nine man crew of the OTTAWA ate and turned in early. They were all in bed by 7:00 for what they thought would be a long and well-deserved sleep. It was not to be, however. At 7:30 the crew was awakened by a huge fire on board, already blazing out of control. The fire had gained such headway that any effort to extinguish it would have been futile, and all the men could do was save themselves. Having virtually no time to even gather up any possessions, the crew ran onto the deck looking for escape. They found it by leaping onto the vessel that they had just saved, which was tied up alongside the flaming OTTAWA. With all men safely aboard the HOYT, the lines to the tug were cut. The boats which had assisted the OTTAWA in the salvage operation then got underway and "it was an easy matter to push the burning OTTAWA from the HOYT. The HOYT was at no time in danger of burning."[2]

News of the terrible accident was immediately sent to Bayfield, and the tug REID was dispatched to the scene. By the time the boat reached the burning OTTAWA however, it was far

The OTTAWA working the SEVONA wreck. Bayfield Heritage Association

too late. The entire vessel was engulfed in flames down to the waterline. She burned for a while longer, then settled and sank.

The origin of the fire remained a mystery, but the assumption was that it had been caused by spontaneous combustion in the coal bunkers. At the time of the blaze the OTTAWA was known to have approximately 130 tons of coal in the hold. The loss of the vessel, with its specialized wrecking machinery, was estimated to be $60,000. She was insured for $40,000. The engine and some machinery were eventually salvaged.

The bones of the once-mighty tug lay in twenty feet of water near the northern edge of Red Cliff Bay. Some of the tug's plankings protrude up to just a couple feet beneath the waters surface, approximately twenty five yards from shore. The remains basically lie parallel to the abandoned H.D. COF-FINBERRY, which sits on shore. The scattered pieces of the OTTAWA belie the fact that she was once one of the most powerful tugs on the Great Lakes. It seems appropriate though, that Captain James Reid's favorite boat went down to fire only after saving one last ship in November of 1909...

Footnotes

1. Red Cliff Bay is also known as Schooner Bay.
2. DULUTH NEWS TRIBUNE, Nov. 30, 1909.
3. It has been erroneously reported in several publications that the scene of the accident was Frog Bay. The entire event happened at Red Cliff Bay.

HERRING KING
Small Boat Tragedy

Superior seamen have always been aware of the great potential for danger while on the water. Fires, fog and storms are obviously very capable candidates for disaster. In this respect, every vessel is alike; no captain is truly exempt from possible tragedy. Small boat skippers operating around the Apostles have had their fair share of anxious moments. The story of the HERRING KING illustrates the point well. On a relatively calm day in 1917 the ill-fated fishing tug literally became a funeral pyre.

Late in the afternoon on November 29th Captain John Gordon was bringing the HERRING KING back to Bayfield. It had been a good day and the boat was loaded down with fish. Just off of Sand Island however, the luck turned bad. Without warning, the KING'S cranky engine sputtered and backfired, and the boat was suddenly on fire. Evidently a fuel line had broken, sending gasoline throughout the bilge. In what seemed like seconds an uncontrollable blaze took command of the KING. The vessel's engineer, Clarence Russell, later remembered:

> The gasoline engine backfired and the flames seemed to spread over the boat all at once. As soon as I saw the flames I sounded the distress signal. There was no way to lower a lifeboat from HERRING KING. The flames spread too rapidly.[1]

Both men were driven to the bow of the boat, the only portion not yet on fire. Their options were quickly becoming increasingly simple: face the flames or the icy cold waters. In the distance they spotted what might be salvation though. A small steamer was evidently speeding to the rescue — the distress signals were heard! Hopefully there would be enough time...

The sixty five foot packet steamer GOLDISH which had been anchored two miles away, had indeed heard the signal and was on its way. Captain S.L. Goldish of Duluth, along with Charles Ljoquist from Two Harbors and Ashland native Eugene Michaud, were no strangers to Apostle Island rescues. The previous year they had saved a Red Cliff man, his family and their boat from certain death in high seas. On another occasion in 1916 the three man crew risked their own lives by going to the aid of the C.W. TURNER, a Booth Company boat. The rescue took hours in a terrible snowstorm but the TURNER and its thirteen crewmembers arrived safely in Bayfield — thanks only to the GOLDISH. Hopefully, another successful rescue was at hand...[2]

Captain Goldish maneuvered his boat as close as possible to the starboard side of the burning vessel. In fact, if the KING'S fuel tanks exploded the GOLDISH — a mere thirty feet away — would very likely become a ball of flame herself. Lifelines were immediately tossed out, but there seemed to be hesitation on the part of the KING'S men to abandon their vessel. Captain Gordon yelled for Russell to jump, but that it would be no use for he himself to try, because he didn't think he could make it. Russell leaped into the freezing water, swam to a lifeline, and was successfully pulled aboard the GOLDISH. The men now anxiously pleaded with Gordon to jump. Finally the flames drove him off the boat, "and he swam towards a life buoy. He seemed to become bewildered

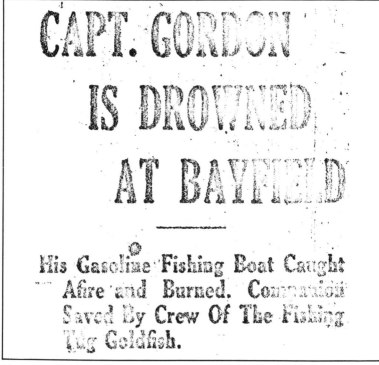

Newspaper headline concerning HERRING KING tragedy.

122

however, when about five feet from the buoy and sank, never appearing again."[3]

The GOLDISH could do nothing else but evacuate the fiery scene. Clarence Russell was taken to the hospital, treated for shock and later released. The body of Captain Gordon "had not been recovered when darkness fell. He is survived by his widow and six children," all of LaPointe.[4] The HERRING KING burned to the waterline and sank. Owned by the S.L. Boutin Fish Company of Bayfield, the vessel was worth $1500, with her cargo valued at $1000. Later, the wreck was towed to the east side of Sand Island, with some machinery and timbers being salvaged.

Captain Goldish and his crew had once again come to the aid of some fellow seamen desperately in need of help. I.R. Nye of Bayfield, who watched the whole accident from shore, put it simply: "The little GOLDISH did noble work in going to the rescue...The crew deserves lots of credit."[5]

Footnotes
1. ASHLAND DAILY PRESS, Nov. 30, 1917.
2. For further information on the GOLDISH and her career, see the excellent article "A Coastal Packet on Lake Superior" by Julius F. Wolff Jr. printed in "INLAND SEAS" Fall 1966.
3. ASHLAND DAILY PRESS, Nov. 30, 1917.
4. Ibid.
5. Ibid.

ONTARIO
The Prohibition Wreck

The last bona fide shipwreck to have occurred in Apostle Island waters was the Canadian barge ONTARIO. She went down in rough seas in October 1927 enroute to Ashland. A unique vessel, a near drowning and an incredible rescue all serve to make this event an interesting tale. Also interesting is the secret cargo that the ONTARIO carried from Canada. For this was the great prohibition era in the U.S., and many people still liked to whet their whistle now and then. After all, what better way than by boat to bring in ten cases of "top-shelf" scotch?

The ONTARIO was built in 1890 of steel construction. She measured 297 feet in length, and had a 1620 net tonnage. Originally used as a barge on the lower lakes she later ran for many years as a car ferry between Detroit and Windsor Ontario. Around 1920 the Newago Tug Line purchased the vessel to haul pulpwood between Port Arthur (Thunder Bay) and Ashland. Captained by Ralph Fromholtz, she was crewed by Elmer Stroshane (fireman), Ernest Ludwig (fireman), Joe Mitchell (fireman and wheelman), and Richard Malek (wheelman). All five men were from Ashland.

On the morning of October 12th the ONTARIO left Port Arthur under tow of the mighty tug BUTTERFIELD. Her cargo consisted of 1100 tons of pulpwood, a heavy load which made the vessel ride low in the water. A stiff northwest wind was blowing when the boats left port, and high waves were beginning to churn. Sizing up the situation, Captain Fromholtz elected to rig a 200 foot long lifeline on board, which extended from the aft cabins to the bow. This proved to be a very wise decision.

As the vessels entered the open lake, the storm grew in intensity. It was not uncommon for waves to wash over the ONTARIO'S deck, but this began to happen consistently with great force. Midway across Superior the situation was becoming increasingly critical. Fireman Ernest Ludwig later recalled:

We were overloaded. There were tons of the five pound pieces of pressed pulpwood even on the deck. When we

A postcard of the ONTARIO.   C. Patrick Labadie Collection

reached about halfway to Ashland, most of it had been washed overboard.[1]

The gale increased in fury, and the treacherous crossing continued. Crewmembers periodically fought the crashing waves to make sure all hatch covers were securely fastened. The ONTARIO began taking on water anyway however, and the swamped boilers finally gave out. The vessel was now without operable pumps or steering power. The BUTTERFIELD was one of the largest tugs on the lake, but towing a zigzagging, partially submerged barge in high seas proved a difficult task. As night fell the tug and tow still managed to plow on though.

Sometime after 2:30 a.m. October 13th fireman Stroshane reported that the water level on deck was almost reaching the galley window. Captain Fromholtz then noticed that water was pouring in the anchor hawseholes. Suddenly the bow lifted and the stern ominously began to lower into the lake. Fromholtz quickly gave orders to prepare the lifeboat, don life preservers and send distress signals to the tug. The lifeboat's lines were cut, but the huge waves immediately washed her overboard. Lanterns were used to signal the BUTTERFIELD, just as the barge's red and green running lights were extinguished by the seas. The vessels were very close to Outer Island, but time was running out for the ONTARIO. At 2:55 the BUTTERFIELD received the distress signals. What happened in the next ten minutes is an incredible story of luck and courage.

Captain Ryerse aboard the BUTTERFIELD immediately checked speed and ordered the 1800 foot towline taken in. As the tug neared her consort, the ONTARIO men made themselves ready.

Leaving the sternhouse the crew had to wade in knee deep water. Clinging to the lifeline in single file, the crew went forward in now waist deep water. The water aft soon reached the top of the sternhouse as the BUTTERFIELD approached them. The forward end was slightly raised. Suddenly the air pressure from the sinking vessel blew up the forward companion or hatch through which the conveyor was always lowered in unloading. The explosion threw wood pulp clear onto the BUTTERFIELD. The BUTTERFIELD crewmembers heard noise of the other manholes being blown onto the deck from air pressure of the sinking vessel.[2]

After bringing in the few remaining feet of the towline, the BUTTERFIELD turned and pulled up alongside the ONTARIO. The barge's crew was huddled in the extreme forward end anxiously waiting. Four of the men were pulled onto the tug, while Ernest Ludwig prepared to axe the two inch towing cable. A lifeline was thrown to him, and in one swing of his blade he freed the sinking vessel. The ONTARIO then literally dropped from under his feet!

Clinging on to a wet and slippery rope, Ludwig hung suspended in midair. The swirling vortex of the sinking ship was incredibly powerful, but Ludwig bravely held on. The men on the BUTTERFIELD pulled the lifeline with all their might, and the terrified fireman was finally swung over to the side of the

The powerful tug BUTTERFIELD which was towing the ONTARIO when she went down.   Bayfield Heritage Association

tug. Banging his head against the stern fender, he lost consciousness for a split second, but Captain Fromholtz managed to grab his ankle. A soaked and scared Ludwig was finally hauled aboard the BUTTERFIELD with only minor cuts and bruises.

Under the nightmarish circumstances the entire rescue was literally unbelievable. The Ashland newspaper reported the following:

> As Ludwig was pulled over the side of the BUTTERFIELD, Captain Ryerse signalled for full speed ahead, but as the barge went down the suction drew the BUTTERFIELD directly over it and the tug was unable to go forward until the suction subsided... The BUTTERFIELD received the distress signal from the barge at 2:55 a.m. The barge sank at 3:05 a.m. There was not a minute to spare. It was even a matter of seconds. If the barge had sunk ten seconds earlier, or if the BUTTERFIELD had lost any time, the crew of the barge would have sunk when it went down.[3]

With ample doses of courage and luck the rescue was successful. The big tug steamed into Ashland and reported the loss. The ONTARIO, worth approximately $25,000, and its $30,000 cargo were both insured. For curiosity's sake the ONTARIO's life preservers were tested a few days after the accident. The crew tied rocks to them and then tossed them all into the lake... only to watch every one of them sink!

Ernest Ludwig made one more trip on a barge, but decided to end his sailing days while he was still ahead. A confirmed "landlubber," the lucky Ludwig never went to sea again. Nothing of course, was saved from the ONTARIO, and she still sits somewhere on the bottom of Superior near Outer Island. And somewhere in the bowels of the prohibition wreck, ten cases of fine scotch still wait to be opened... over half a century later.

Footnotes
1. SUPERIOR EVENING TELEGRAM, February 16, 1978.
2. ASHLAND DAILY PRESS, October 13, 1927.
3. Ibid.

SECTION III
Accidents
Abandonments
Visiting The Vessels

Accidents

The Chequamegon shipping region basically laid claim to twenty one wrecked vessels. A glance at the maritime accidents in the area however indicates that the number of ships that almost sailed their last here is considerably greater. The quantity of minor mishaps and major disasters that occurred in the vicinity also indicate the volume of vessel traffic during the area's shipping heyday.

The following chronological list is a compendium of known accidents around the region. The private yacht mishaps — of which there were (and still are) many — have not been mentioned. Included mainly are the accidents from the great shipping period in the area: some were truly tragic in terms of damage and death, while others were merely "brushes," just enough to keep an unwary captain on his toes.

1883:

ALICE CRAIG
On Friday, November 16th the schooner CRAIG was being towed by a small steamer, bound for Isle Royale. Encountering a gale the vessels ran for shelter in the Apostles. Near Stockton Island the towing cable parted and the CRAIG was blown onto Presque Isle beach. The following day the tug PACIFIC steamed to her aid and succeeded in freeing her. The schooner's steering gear was damaged, but an extra rudder was immediately put in place and she continued on her way.

1884:

S.C. BALDWIN
The teambarge ran aground near Ashland's waterfront. She was easily released with repairs costing $800.
PACIFIC
On the afternoon of August 19th the Union Mill Company tug PACIFIC was docked at the Miller and Richie mill in Ashland when her boilers blew up. The tremendous explosion instantly killed three crewmembers on board, and caused damages amounting to $3000.

N. BOUTIN

On November 24th the 68 foot tug BOUTIN foundered off of Washburn, but was later raised with surprisingly little damage.

1885:

KITTY M. FORBES

On November 6th the steamer FORBES was towing the schooner SHELDON when a vicious northeaster started howling. Both ships were loaded with coal bound for Two Harbors, Minnesota. By nightfall the vessels were in bad shape, but were nearing the Apostles. While attempting to run for shelter the FORBES was mercilessly thrown onto some rocks near Outer Island. The SHELDON'S towing line was immediately cut, in hopes that she could avoid the same fate. The schooner's steering gear failed however, and she drifted helplessly. By sheer luck the SHELDON somehow managed to stay clear of the danger, and was blown into sheltered waters.

Meanwhile the crew of the FORBES had decided that it would be best to purposely scuttle their vessel, to prevent her from being pounded to pieces. They literally "pulled the plug" and braved the high seas in lifeboats. Two days later the FORBES crew miraculously rowed into Ashland unharmed. That same afternoon the tug R.W. CURRIE from Bayfield discovered the SHELDON still drifting safely, and towed her into port.

The SHELDON'S steering gear was quickly repaired and she sailed on to Duluth. The owners of the FORBES ordered a steam pump from Chicago to deal with their problem. After two weeks, great expense and much difficulty the FORBES was finally raised. The repairs cost a hefty $16,200.

FAVORITE

The schooner FAVORITE departed Ashland during a terrible storm after picking up a load of iron ore. She immediately encountered great difficulties and eventually foundered just off Bayfield's waterfront. The vessel was later raised with damages amounting to $5000.

1889:

AUSTRALASIA

At 11:00 p.m. April 23rd the steamer ran aground on Michigan Island while seeking shelter from a northeast gale. She was eventually released but had suffered extensive damage. Repairs cost the owners approximately $12,000.

A.C. ADAMS, MONTEREY

On June 19th the tug ADAMS with the schooner MONTEREY in tow grounded on Sand Island. Both vessels were released with a sum total of damages amounting to $1500.

1890:

HUNTER

A minor mishap occurred when the 134 foot Booth Company steamer broke her wheel while backing away from an Ashland dock. Repairs cost $375.

IRON RING

While discharging coal at an Ashland dock on July 4th the steamer KING took fire. The blaze spread with incredible speed, enveloping the forward cabin and upper deck. No one was injured but the damage was estimated to be a whopping $20,000 worth!

1893:

PRENTICE

On November 16th the steamer PRENTICE and consort MIDDLESEX were making their way through a dense fog. Both vessles were owned by the Shores Lumber Company and were bound for Ashland to pick up cargoes. With zero visibility the PRENTICE ran aground on Outer Island rocks. The schooner in tow avoided the hazard and floated nearby. After thirty six hours of futile efforts the PRENTICE finally freed herself, with relatively little damage done.

1894:

ALVA

On August 8th the steamer ALVA caught fire while moored at Washburn. The blaze was extinguished with no injuries, and damage repairs costing $1000.

1896:

OMAHA

An early summer storm on May 12th sent the steamer OMAHA scurrying for Apostle Island shelter. She was unfortunately thrown onto the east side of Devil's Island instead. The repair bill from damages cost her owners $1500.

1898:

VEGA, BULGARIA

On May 18th the steamer VEGA was towing her usual barge AMAZON and a disabled steamer BULGARIA. The VEGA had picked up the BULGARIA after her steering gear failed near Sault Ste. Marie. All three vessels were carrying coal bound for

Duluth. A strong north wind began blowing that evening and the VEGA impaled itself on Gull Island, with the BULGARIA following suit. High winds and heavy seas pounded the exposed vessels. The Singer Line tugs SUPERIOR and ZENITH of Duluth succeeded in freeing both boats two days later, and towed them to Superior. Repairs to the VEGA cost $20,000, the BULGARIA $3000.

W.H. SAWYER

On September 23rd the steamer SAWYER ran aground on Sand Island during a storm. She was released with nominal damage.

1899:

R.W. CURRIE

While moored at an Ashland dock on September 2nd the 60 foot steamer CURRIE took fire. The flames were quickly brought under control however, and there was little damage.

CITY OF TRAVERSE

On September 28th the steamer TRAVERSE fouled her steering gear near Bayfield. She was towed into port and fitted with a new rudder.

1900:

LIZZIE MADDEN

On November 18th the MADDEN left Ashland with two vessels, the MAUTENEE and NOQUEBAY, in tow. At midnite, while the crews were changing, a fire was discovered below decks. A lamp had tipped over or exploded in the crew's quarters in the forward end, port side. A strong wind enraged the flames, but the crew of fourteen finally managed to control the fire. The damage repairs cost $2000.

1902:

BENNETT

The steamer BENNETT left Bayfield one evening with fifteen crewmembers aboard. The following morning one of the men was inexplicably missing. The official report given by the vessel's officers simply claimed that the man was terribly intoxicated, and must have fallen overboard!

1903:

ELIZA

At Bayfield one crewmember from the tug ELIZA fell overboard and drowned.

1904:

LUCILE

While moored at an Ashland dock a fire broke out on the steamer LUCILE, causing damages worth $600.

1905:

MELVIN S. BACON

On Sunday, September 24th a bad leak was discovered on the 182 foot barge MELVIN S. BACON. She was sitting at the Central Ore dock, after receiving 1,272 tons of ore. Distress signals were blown, as she was taking on water faster than the pumps could handle it. The tug INMAN arrived on the scene, and proceeded to tow the sinking barge away from the oredock, towards the Clarkson Coal Company dock. Two hours later the BACON sank in eighteen feet of water aft, and thirteen feet forward.

That night the crew decided to sleep on board, as their cabins were still "high and dry." At 1:00 a.m. a fire was discovered on the ill-fated BACON, and the men narrowly escaped with their lives. The tug TOM DOWLING quickly came alongside and threw water on the burning barge, but the damage was extensive. The aft section was completely destroyed and the deck was burned straight through.

The original decision of the owners was to salvage the cargo and let the BACON lie. On October 3rd though, they tried to raise the old vessel, and their efforts were successful. The boat was sufficiently patched up to be towed downbound, and repaired at great expense.

WILLIAM E. COREY

The same terrible tempest that sent the IRA OWEN to the bottom almost claimed the huge flagship of the Pittsburgh Steamship Company. The brand new $475,000 COREY was thrown on to Gull Island reef on November 28th. Once aground, the proud vessel endured a terrible beating. A lesser ship probably would not have withstood the pounding, but the COREY somehow remained intact. Efforts to free the "pride of the line" were without precedent in the Apostles. At one time the salvage outfit comprised 158 men, five steamers and three tugs. Success was finally met twelve days after the stranding. The repair bill: An astronomical $100.000!

SIR WILLIAM SIEMENS

While attempting to free the impaled WILLIAM E. COREY, the steamer WILLIAM SIEMENS got hung up on Gull Island reef on December 2nd. The damage repairs cost $5000.

EDNA G.

The famous tug EDNA G. also suffered damage in efforts to

release the WILLIAM E. COREY on December 2nd. While holding up the bow of the big steamer, she was dragged onto Gull Island reef with damages amounting to $1000.

1906:

R.L. IRELAND
On December 7th the 416 foot steamer IRELAND stranded on Gull Island. She was eventually freed, but on her way to Duluth, under tow of the tug CROSBY, she encountered a vicious northeaster which claimed the life of one man. Total damages were estimated at $90,000.

The CORMORANT loaded with lumber. She endured tragedy in 1907.

1907:

CORMORANT
On the morning of October 30th the 218 foot lumber hooker CORMORANT departed Bayfield bound for Duluth. In the west channel she was discovered to be on fire and her captain beached her immediately on Basswood Island. The vessel burned completely to the waterline. She was later towed back to Bayfield where her boilers and some machinery was salvaged. She was virtually a total loss, insured for $10,000.
TOM DOWLING
While breaking through ice near Washburn on December 18th the tug DOWLING ripped a hole in her hull. Punctured

Machinery of the CORMORANT being salvaged in Bayfield.

Bayfield Heritage Association

The boiler of the CORMORANT being salvaged at Bayfield.

Bayfield Heritage Association

clear through, the vessel sank in fourteen feet of water. She was raised and her repair bill luckily only cost approximately $500.

1908:

TOM DOWLING

Only six months after being raised, the tug DOWLING sank again! On June 6th while lying at the Wisconsin Central oredock in Ashland, she inexplicably went down in twenty feet of water. The cause was later discovered to be an open seacock. Another $500 repair bill was sent to the owner.

1909:

E.J. EARLINE

The 535 foot steamer EARLINE stranded on Madeline Island in a heavy fog on May 28. She was later released with $25,000 damage.

JOHN A. DONALDSON

On August 7th a fireman aboard the DONALDSON committed suicide by jumping overboard near Outer Island.

JAMES H. HOYT

A November northeaster sent the 363 foot steamer HOYT running for Apostle Island shelter. She unfortunately ran aground on Outer Island instead. She was later released by the Reid wrecking tug OTTAWA (which was the tug's final job) and towed to shelter. The repairs to the HOYT cost $65,000.

JAMES S. DUNHAM

A late season storm completely wrecked the steering gear on the 424 foot DUNHAM. She ended up stranding between Bad River and Chequamegon Point. The following day she was released and repaired for $2000.

1910:

HAROLD B. NYE

A minor mishap occurred on July 15th at Ashland harbor. The steamer C.O. JENKINS backed into the NYE accidently and damaged her upper works. Cost of repairs was $200.

1911:

A.L. HOPKINS

On October 2nd the 174 foot lumber hooker HOPKINS departed Bayfield fully loaded. At 11:00 p.m., fifteen miles east of Michigan Island, they encountered a tremendous gale

The A.L. HOPKINS. In 1911 she floated for weeks before finally sinking.

which nearly capsized the vessel. Some lumber on deck, along with a crewman were washed overboard. The lifeboat was made ready to launch but was also washed overboard with one man in it. Three hours later the two crewmembers, given up for dead, clambered back on board the disabled vessel! The first man had clung to some floating lumber, and the lifeboat had landed right side up in the water. The following morning the steamer ALVA DINKEY picked up the HOPKINS crew in their lifeboat. The HOPKINS floated bow up for two weeks after she was abandoned, last being seen some fifty five miles northeast of Outer Island. She was a total loss and not insured.

1912:

ONOKO
This accident story begins at Superior harbor when the steamer STADASCONA passed close by the 287 foot ONOKO. It was only a "brush" however, and no damage was done — or so the ONOKO'S captain thought. The vessel left port but when coming up to the Apostles, a bad leak was discovered. The pumps couldn't handle the inrushing water so the ONOKO was purposely grounded. Later investigation showed that the hull had been punctured by the STADASCONA'S propellor. Repairs cost $950.

1914:

JOHN H. BOLAND
While enroute from Fort William to Superior in July the BOLAND lost her way in a dense fog. She stranded on North Twin Island with repairs totalling $6,836.

1917:

P.P. MILLER
On November 8th the 354 foot steamer MILLER was heading for Ashland in a thick fog. On the south end of Madeline Island she struck hard on a shoal and damaged both bow and stern. The vessel limped into port and was repaired for $15,500.

1920:

WILLIAM A. WOLFE
At 11:00 p.m. August 5th a dense Superior fog got the best of the 504 foot WOLFE. She ran hard aground on Devil's Island, but released herself. Damage was extensive however, with repairs totalling $20,000.

1921:

CAPTAIN THOMAS WILSON
Bound for Washburn on May 22nd the 421 foot steamer WILSON stranded on Gull Island in a fog. The infamous little island cost the WILSON'S owners $40,000 in repair bills. Investigation found that the compasses were "deflected by lightning."

1922:

E.S. ROBISON
On October 22nd the coal-laden steamer ran aground on the east side of a fog-filled Devils Island. She was freed and continued on to her destination of Duluth. Repairs cost $20,000.

1924:

JOHN W. AILES
During an August 22nd storm the steamer AILES ran aground on Rocky Island while seeking shelter. Released the next day, the repair bill was $20,000.

1928:
BROCKTON
On October 15th while enroute from Duluth to Buffalo, the steamer BROCKTON struck an obstruction off of Devil's Island. She was towed back to Duluth with damage to her rudder and propellor costing $3000.

1929:
MARIGOLD
A freak accident took place on October 2nd, killing three men. The government boat MARIGOLD was moored at a light buoy off of Red Cliff point. A lighthouse tender was replacing the contents of an acetylene tank which furnished the light, when it blew up with tremendous force. The tender was literally "blown to bits," while a second man was hurled against the vessel's mast and a third flew right off the boat. All three were killed instantly.

ABANDONMENTS

Any area that has experienced a great deal of shipping activity inevitably contains her share of abandonments. Like thoroughbreds put out to pasture all vessels must eventually face the boneyard. The following list contains the known abandonments in the Apostle Islands/Chequamegon Bay region. Some simply died of old age, some were victims of economic misfortune, and others basically outlived their usefulness. Most were stripped and scuttled, salvaged and forgotten.

It is highly unlikely that the list is fully complete. There have simply been too many small vessels (private yachts, fishing boats, scows, etc.) operating in the area over the years to make that claim. Besides those listed there have been reports of two unidentified tugs near Bayfield, three vessels in Raspberry Bay, a fishing boat near Barksdale and perhaps others depending on which local mariner you talk to.

Ashland Area:
HAZEL

This was a prominent little tug on Chequamegon waters around the turn of the century. Owned and operated by Captain I.H. Maxim, the sturdy little steamer was used mainly for rafting logs. The vessel was simply abandoned when Maxim moved to Park Falls. The remains lie near shore just east of the Soo Line ore dock in Ashland.

MADELINE

This vessel was originally named the BRUCE. Under both titles the steamer was used as a ferry/excursion boat on the bay and around the islands. A busy career ended when she was abandoned in shallow water just east of the Soo Line ore dock, very close to the HAZEL.

EMERALD

The famous sidewheeler was abandoned at W.R. Durfee's dock in 1893. The vessel was built in 1862 at Algomac Michigan for L.S. Bowtell. She was 150 feet long, 40 feet wide with a 9 foot depth and listed a 215 gross tonnage. Originally used as a packet steamer around the Great Lakes, the EMERALD was brought to the bay area in the 1880's. Here she was used in a variety of ways: making regular trips to the north

The sidewheeler EMERALD loaded with passengers.

shore and back, towing logs for different lumber companies, and taking excursionists around the islands.

The EMERALD was a popular local boat, but perhaps she is best remembered for her final two voyages — to Lake Huron. In 1892 the owner, W.R. Durfee, fitted her out as a dive/salvage vessel. A Superior man, Oliver Pelkey (formerly of Ashland), had invented and tested a deep sea diving suit, and the two men had decided to make some money for themselves. They intended to find the famous shipwreck PEWABIC, and hopefully raise her cargo — including 300 tons of copper bars worth $300,000, and $75,000 in silver in the ship's strongbox. The PEWABIC had gone down in 1864 with seventy people killed.

In October the EMERALD set out for Huron and the lost ship. upon arrival, the men miraculously found the PEWABIC almost immediately. Pelkey donned his 780 pound diving suit and verified the find. She was sitting in 131 feet of water. After coming up for more weight, Pelkey descended again . . . for the last time. Against orders he climbed inside the wreckage and got hung up. When the tenders finally brought the diver up via his lifeline, they discovered what happened: his suit got

Another view of the EMERALD, abandoned in 1893.

caught on something, ripped open, and Pelkey drowned. The EMERALD returned to Ashland.

The following year another trip was planned, complete with new diver and new suit. After four months of futile searching for the PEWABIC however the sidewheeler returned home and was moored for the last time. So ended the "Ashland Expeditions," and the EMERALD'S career. The abandoned remains lie in shallow water just west of the Lake Superior District Power plant in Ashland.

Pikes Bay (Port Superior):
CHARLOTTE

The fishing tug CHARLOTTE was dragged to her final resting place in 1943. The 65 foot steamer was abandoned there after putting in many good years of service around the islands. The remains lie in shallow water just south of the Port Superior marina. She can be seen from shore partially sticking out of the water.

Barge

The remains of a flat bottomed scow lie partially out of the water just to the north of the Port Superior marina. The barge used to carry a boom on her deck for transfer of cargo, and often was towed by the tug ASHLAND (now resting in Red Cliff

Bay) earlier in this century. She was abandoned in the 1930's, and fire has since gutted her.

Bayfield Area:
FINN McCOOL

The steam barge FINN McCOOL (named after a legendary giant in Irish folklore) sits in twenty feet of water near the Apostle Islands Yacht Club. The vessel was built in 1927 in Ashland for the John Schroeder Lumber Company. Built of white oak, the boat sported a two story deckhouse, large work boom, black smokestack and steam winch. She measured 135 feet long, 34 feet wide, 7.7 feet deep and 343 gross tons. The FINN McCOOL was used mainly for lumber transport around the islands and other south shore points.

The steamer changed hands seven times before she was abandoned in 1964. Sitting at a Bayfield slip one night, loaded with Oak Island logs, her pumps failed and she unceremoniously sank at the dock. Her cargo was salvaged and the ferries GAR HOW and NICHEVO dragged her to her final resting place. She is still relatively intact, and can be seen partially sticking out of the water.

ANDERSON

The tug was simply left to rot earlier in the century at a Bayfield dock. She sat at the foot of Washington Avenue, where today there is a public beach. The old fishing boat is nowhere in sight, however, having been completely covered by the sand a short distance from shore.

The FINN McCOOL with tug BAYFIELD alongside it.

Bayfield Heritage Association

The FINN McCOOL loaded down with logs. Bayfield Heritage Association

Red Cliff Bay (Schooner Bay):
ASHLAND
The tug ASHLAND, formerly the A.C. VAN RAALTE, had a long career in the bay area. She was built in Buffalo, New York in 1867, and her final owner was the John Schroeder Lumber Company. The little steamer was a victim of the depression and abandoned in the early 1930's. She laid on the beach at Ashland for a short period of time, but was later salvaged and towed to Red Cliff Bay.
H.D. COFFINBERRY
The bulk freighter COFFINBERRY was built in 1874 at East Saginaw, Michigan. Thomas Arnold constructed the wooden steamer for Rust, King and Company of Cleveland. The vessel measured 191.4 feet long, 33.5 feet wide, 13.4 feet deep and 858 gross tons. She was originally used for hauling iron ore, but later was adapted for the lumber trade. The big steamer simply outlived her usefulness and was abandoned in 1913. She lies partially on shore at the north side of Red Cliff Bay.
R.W. CURRIE
The 60 foot CURRIE was a well-known steam tug, used extensively in the area around the turn of the century. She took part in many rescues around the islands, one of which included picking up the stranded Sand Island survivors from the SEVONA wreck of 1905. She was laid to rest in Red Cliff Bay some years later. Her remains lie partially on shore, very near the H.D. COFFINBERRY.

Outer Island:
FAITHFUL

The small steamer FAITHFUL carried on quite a diversified career in the region. She was used for awhile as a fishing tug, but later converted to a car/passenger ferry. She was abandoned in shallow water near the south end of Outer Island in 1950. Today a sand spit extends out to the scuttled tug.

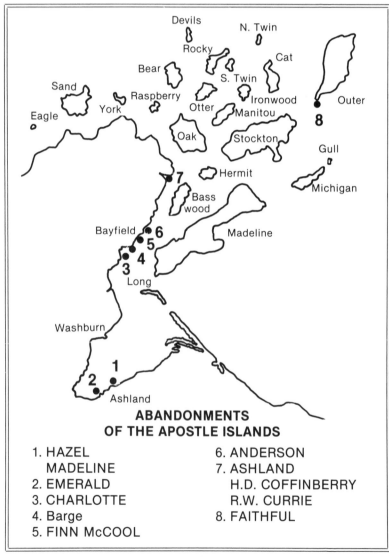

ABANDONMENTS
OF THE APOSTLE ISLANDS

1. HAZEL
   MADELINE
2. EMERALD
3. CHARLOTTE
4. Barge
5. FINN McCOOL

6. ANDERSON
7. ASHLAND
   H.D. COFFINBERRY
   R.W. CURRIE
8. FAITHFUL

The bones of the H.D. COFFINBERRY lie in Red Cliff Bay.

The S.B. BARKER (left) and the R.W. CURRIE at Bayfield. The CURRIE remains sit at Red Cliff Bay.

VISITING THE VESSELS

The dead ships that lay scattered about the Apostle Islands area have obviously sailed into history, but many can still be visited today. Some are basically on shore and others can be seen partially sticking out of the water. Mask, fins and snorkel can provide the interested person with a greater opportunity for wreck examination, while scuba gear can be the key to much further firsthand exploration.[1]

Many of the abandoned vessels can be seen lying on or near shore.[2] The remains of the three Red Cliff Bay boats, the R.W. CURRIE, H.D. COFFINBERRY and ASHLAND, all basically lie out of the water. The hull of the COFFINBERRY can be easily spotted, for instance, offering a glimpse of 1870's construction methods. On Outer Island the sand spit has grown so much in recent decades that the scuttled FAITHFUL will soon be part of the island. In Sand Island's East Bay the remains of the HERRING KING lay near shore. After she burned and sank the hull was towed to the present location and salvaged, so there isn't much of the old fishing boat left. The forgotten FINN McCOOL near Bayfield and the Pikes Bay abandonments all partially break the water's surface, as does the wrecked FEDORA at Red Cliff.[3]

With snorkeling gear some of the vessels can be checked out quite thoroughly. An interesting skin dive for example, is the FEDORA. The ship was burned to the waterline and later salvaged, but the ribs and planking from stem to stern are still there for the most part. The relatively intact FINN McCOOL is a worthwhile snorkeling excursion. Much of the boat's machinery is still on deck or scattered nearby. The bones of the NOQUE BAY in Stockton Island's Julian Bay lie in shallow water just off the beach. The vessel was badly burned, but some of the hull structure still remains. Another burn victim, the recently discovered R.G. STEWART, lies close to shore at Michigan Island.

More wrecks are available to explore with the aid of scuba equipment. The FINN McCOOL, for instance, is a dive well worth the effort. The vessel, resting in ten to twenty feet of water, offers the diver opportunities for easy penetration. The big tug OTTAWA, which burned in Red Cliff Bay, can be visited with scuba. Much of the boat is still there, but it is badly broken up. She lies almost parallel to the H.D. COFFINBERRY, about twenty five yards from shore with a maximum depth of twenty five feet. On a calm day the LUCERNE wreck off of Long Island is a good dive destination. Portions of the intact hull remain, but most of the machinery and artifacts have been brought up over the years.[4] The remains of the R.G. STEWART near Michigan Island lie in fifteen feet of water, maximum depth, and can easily be "scuba'd."

The two September 1905 shipwrecks — the SEVONA and PRETORIA are excellent dive sites. The SEVONA on Sand Island shoals was dynamited in 1909 so pieces of her are widely scattered. Small artifacts, such as silverware and personal belongings still occasionally turn up however, uncovered by the shifting sand. Both anchors from the vessel were recovered some years ago, and one of them is on display at the National Lakeshore headquarters at Little Sand Bay. The PRETORIA sits less than a mile off the northeast end of Outer Island. For decades she has been victimized by Superior's openwater gales however, and pieces of her are badly strewn about. The anchors from the big ship were brought up, and can be seen at the museum on Madeline Island.

The number of shipwrecks in the area is obviously greater than the list of vessels mentioned here. In other words, many of the ships that went down in these waters have not yet been found. Some are undoubtedly in very deep water, while others — if discovered — would definitely be visitable. A few of the undiscovered wrecks, like the CITY OF ASHLAND and the PRUSSIA, are probably little more than burned-out hulls, but others must certainly be in near perfect condition. Those that foundered without burning would be very interesting discoveries. The cargo and contents of many of the dead vessels would, of course, be worth a considerable sum of money. Perhaps more importantly, however, would be the inestimable value in terms of history and education. A piece of a past culture could be studied and analyzed.

Firsthand research of Lake Superior shipwrecks has a unique, valuable quality attached to it. The preservative powers of the big lake are virtually nonpareil. Vessel deterioration and decay progress at an incredibly slow rate in the clean, cold freshwater. With little plant life or pollution, no coral or barnacles, Superior's dead ships are seemingly frozen in time. The undiscovered Apostle Island wrecks could potentially be considered a veritable museum of maritime antiquity. In short, Lake Superior preserves well what she has claimed from man.[5]

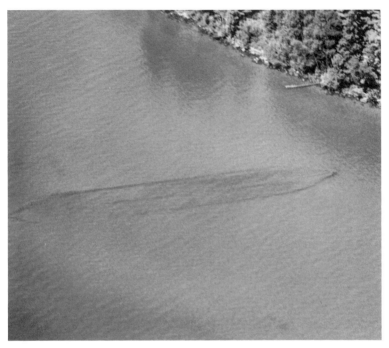

Aerial view of the FEDORA.

Footnotes

1. It should be mentioned that Lake Superior is rarely, if ever, comfortably warm. If snorkeling or scuba diving, a wetsuit is usually a necessity.

2. The three abandoned vessels in Ashland lie close to shore, but the water visibility there is virtually always next to nothing. Viewing any parts of the EMERALD, MADELINE or HAZEL is therefore usually impossible.

3. Caution should be exercised when boating near these vessels!

4. The Canal Park Marine Museum in Duluth has an excellent display of artifacts from the LUCERNE.

5. If planning to visit the vessels within the Apostle Island National Lakeshore waters, consult the park service people at the Bayfield headquarters first. National Lakeshore waters extend one quarter of a mile out from all park shores, and at the present time a permit is needed to visit all "underwater archaelogical sites." It it against park service policy to take items off the vessels, and "wreck raping" will not be tolerated!

BIBLIOGRAPHY

"Ashland Daily Press' 1887-1979.

"Ashland News" 1883-1893.

"Ashland Weekly Press' 1883-1886.

Barry, James P., **Ships of the Great Lakes,** Howell North Books: San Diego, Calif., 1973.

Barry, James P., **Wrecks and Rescues of the Great Lakes,** Howell North Books: San Diego, Calif., 1981.

"Bayfield County Press" 1883-1927.

Beeson, Harvey C., **Inland Marine Directory,** 1887-1915.

Boyer, Dwight, **True Tales of the Great Lakes,** Dodd, Mead and Company: New York, N.Y., 1971.

Boyer, Dwight, **Strange Adventures of the Great Lakes,** Dodd, Mead and Company: New York, N.Y., 1974.

Burnham, Guy M., **The Lake Superior Country In History And In Story,** Edwards Brothers: Ann Arbor, Michigan, 1929.

"Detroit Free Press" 1883.

"Duluth Herald" 1897-1909.

"Duluth News Tribune" 1885-1917.

Engman, Elmer, **Shipwreck Guide to the Western Half of Lake Superior,** Inner Space: Duluth, Minnesota, 1979.

Hatcher, Harlan, **The Great Lakes,** Oxford University Press, New York, N.Y., 1944.

Harris, Walt, **The Chequamegon Country,** Walter J. Harris: Fayetteville, Arkansas, 1976.

"Inland Seas" Fall 1966.

Maritime Research and Publishing Co., **Treasure Ships of the Great Lakes,** Maritime Research and Publishing Co.: Detroit, Michigan, 1981.

Merchant Vessels of the United States (Annual List), U.S. Department of Transportation: Washington D.C., 1885-1964.

Polk, R.L., **Marine Directory of the Great Lakes,** Polk and Company: Detroit, Michigan, 1891.

"Port Huron Daily Times" 1893.

Ratigan, William, **Great Lakes Shipwrecks and Survivals,** William B. Eerdmans Publishing Co.: Grand Rapids, Michigan, 1977.

Stonehouse, Frederick, **Went Missing,** Avery Color Studies: Autrain, Michigan, 1977.

"'Superior Evening Telegram" 1978.

Wells, Homer, **History of Accidents, Casualties, and Wrecks on Lake Superior,** U.S. Army Corps of Engineers: Duluth, Minnesota, 1938.

Wolff, Dr. Julius F. Jr., **The Shipwrecks of Lake Superior,** Lake Superior Marine Museum Association Inc.: Duluth, Minnesota, 1979.

VESSEL INDEX

For additional copies contact:

APOSTLE ISLAND PRESS
P.O. Box 751
Bayfield, Wisconsin 54814